TWO MORE STEPS

TWO MORE STEPS

638 More Quotations *for* Runners

to Make You Laugh *and* Lace Up Your Shoes

Selected, compiled, and some even written by

RANDY L. THURMAN

Master Key Publications

Master Key Publications
Oklahoma City, Oklahoma

Cover design by Damonza
Illustrations by Byan S. Wibawanto

ISBN: 978-1-948607-10-0

This book is dedicated to Joe Warfield, Boston marathoner and friend. His life was cut short when he was hit by a truck while on a 10-mile run. The Joltin' Joe 5k is now put on every November in Oklahoma City to honor him and raise awareness about driver safety.

Thanks for the inspiration, Joe.

1

To give anything less than your best is to sacrifice the gift.

—Steve Prefontaine, a running legend who died at the age of 24, but already held every American record in distances from 2,000 to 10,000 meters and 2 to 6 miles

(*This is one of my all-time favorite quotes—so great that it's the only one that appears both here and in my first book of quotations,* One More Step: 638 Quotations for Runners to Entertain and Inspire you)

2

How do you run a marathon? It's like life, you take one more step to your goal and repeat.

> –Advice overheard from a marathoner to a non-runner

3

A Runner's Prayer
I pray that I may run
Until my dying day.

And when it comes to my last race,
I then most humbly pray,

When checking in for the Lord's great race,
And standing there a sinner,

That God in His mercy finds me
Qualified to enter.

> –Randy L. Thurman

4

Running teaches us to keep moving forward one step at a time, especially in the most painful moments.

> –Unknown

5

Never give up, never give up. Never, ever give up.

> –Jim Valvano, former coach of the North Carolina State championship basketball team, in an impassioned speech about his battle with cancer
>
> (*If you've never seen it, it's a must watch. Google it.*)

6

I often solved problems as I ran. The kind of thinking I most like to do while I run, though, is just to let my thoughts wander wherever they wish.

> –Jim Fixx, helped popularize the sport of running by demonstrating its health benefits, author of the classic *The Complete Book of Running*

7

Running is the only time my mind is quiet. Probably because I'm focused on not falling down.

> –Unknown

8

If someone says to you, "You can't run a..." whatever it is, tell him or her, "Yes, I can. You're not going to stop me, not this time. This is too important. I want to do this thing. I want to set a clear goal for myself and achieve it. I know I can, and I will. With your help or without it. Now if you'll just shut your trap, I'm going to go for a run.

> -Kevin Nelson, from his inspirational book *The Runner's Book of Daily Inspiration*

9

The only one who can tell you "you can't" is you. And you don't have to listen.

> -Nike

10

I'll be happy if running and I can grow old together.

> -Haruki Murakami, a writer with bestsellers in Japan as well as internationally, in *What I Talk About When I Talk About Running: A Memoir*

11

Son, it don't take long to live a lifetime.

–Leo Thurman, age 81, talking about life, and when you should start doing the things you need and want to do.

(*Leo Thurman was my dad, who gave me a lifetime of love and wisdom.*)

12

To keep your motivation high, use mental stimuli. Find out what gets you psyched, and surround yourself with it; posters, sayings, photos, running magazines, videos.

–Grete Waitz, Norwegian marathon runner and former world record holder

13

At age 43, when I found myself standing in the garage in my new pair of running shoes, I knew that it was my moment of truth.... Behind me lay 40 years of bad decisions and broken promises.

–John "the penguin" Bingham, *The Courage to Start*

14

There are many challenges to long distance running, but one of the greatest is the question of where to put the car keys.

> –Gabrielle Zevin, American Author and screen-writer.

15

Resolve says, "I will." The man says, "I will climb this mountain. They told me it was too high, too far, too steep, too rocky and too difficult. But it is my mountain. I will climb it. You will soon see me waving from the top or dead on the side from trying."

> –Jim Rohn, entrepreneur, business philosopher, success coach, and author of more than thirty books, including *The Art of Exceptional Living*

> (*How's your resolve?*)

16

Pain is inevitable. Suffering is optional.

> –Haruki Murakami, a writer with bestsellers in Japan as well as internationally, in *What I Talk About When I Talk About Running*

17

Running is not just exercise; it's a lifestyle.

> –John Bingham, in *Running for Mortals: A Commonsense Plan for Changing Your Life Through Running*

18

I don't run to add days to my life, I run to add life to my days.

> –Ronald Rook, a Vermont author, naturalist, and Vermont Public Radio commentator

19

You're never too old to set another goal or dream a new dream.

> –C.S. Lewis, Christian apologist, novelist, and medievalist

20

You must take personal responsibility. You cannot change the circumstances, the seasons, or the wind, but you can change yourself. That is something you can have charge of.

> –Jim Rohn, entrepreneur, business philosopher, success coach, and author of more than thirty books, including *7 Strategies for Wealth & Happiness: Power Ideas from America's Foremost Business Philosopher*

21

Running will welcome you, no matter how highly incapable you've been at sports. Give it a chance to do that.

> –Dana L. Ayers in *Confessions of an Unlikely Runner: A Guide to Racing and Obstacle Courses for the Averagely Fit and Halfway Dedicated*

22

We often think that motivation is what we need to get us going, but motivation is not the beginning of the process, it's the result of something else; the "why."

> –Michelle Segar Ph.D. University of Michigan, motivational scientist and author of *No Sweat*
>
> (*In other words...start with why.*)

23

I'll be thinking about my daughter the whole time.

-Stella Denniss, who ran five marathons in five days to raise funds for her daughter, who has hypotonia

(*Note: Beware of donating on a per-mile basis!*)

24

For me it's about finishing lines, not finishing times.

-Vickie Humber, who wore a size 32 when started running and is now a size 16

25

The ability to see myself as more capable and independent than I'd imagined I could be.

-Emma Rorke, a runner, when asked, "What's the greatest gift running has given you?"

26

Dopamine!

> –Lauren S. Tashma, PhD mental performance coach at Align Performance, when asked for a reason to run; she went on to explain, "It's the happy chemical and gets released in our brains as a reward when we do something good."

27

Not finishing and coming in last had been my two greatest fears. But when I realized the latter virtually guarantees you a standing ovation, and that you get the same medal as the person who came first, I was never afraid of it again.

> –Lisa Jackson, who has finished dead last in 25 of her 106 marathons

28

Running isn't a sport for pretty boys.... It's about the sweat in your hair and the blisters on your feet. It's the frozen spit on your chin and the nausea in your gut. It's about throbbing calves and cramps at midnight that are strong enough to wake the dead. It's about getting out the door and running when the rest of the world is only dreaming about having the passion that you need to live each and every day with.

> –Paul Maurer, a German footballer who plays as a right winger for FSV Union Fürstenwalde

29

Stay strong, love yourself, and do what you need to do, not what you want to do.

> –Ida Keeling, who set the 100-meter record in the 100 to 104 age division, when asked by *Runner's World* magazine what advice she had for younger runners; author of *Can't Nothing Bring Me Down: Chasing Myself in the Race against Time*

30

Runner's recruiting motto:

Give me your heavy footed, your less than nimble.

Your couch potatoes yearning to be in shape.

The woefully inactive in their reclining chairs.

Send these, the apprehensive and uncertain among us.

We'll guide you joyfully into your comfortable running groove!

> –Bob Schwartz, in *I Run, Therefore I Am—Nuts!*

31

The most important thing I learned is that there is only one runner in this race, and that is me.

> –George Sheehan, physician, senior athlete, and author of many great books, including *Running & Being: The Total Experience*; when asked, in the last days of his life, "What's the single most important thing running has taught you about life?"

32

I saw my injury as an opportunity.

> –Rob Jones, who lost his legs to an IED in Afghanistan and later ran 31 marathons in 31 days in 31 cities with two above-the-knee running blades

33

I had a stroke, have a hole in my heart, and have brain damage—but as long as I'm breathing, I'll still be running.

> –Ronnie Staton, coach and motivational speaker

34

Keep your dream in front of you. Never let it go regardless of how far-fetched it might seem.

–Hal Higdon, author of more than 36 books, in *Marathoning A to Z*

35

I run slower than a turtle going through peanut butter, but I still run.

–Message printed on a runner's shirt

36

Leg or not, nothing was going to stop me from my dreams.

–Amy Palmiero, who lost her leg in a motorcycle accident and later held world records in twelve different events, including a 100-mile ultra-marathon

37

If you go to work on your goals, your goals will work on you. If you work on your plan, your plan will go to work on you. Whatever good things we build end up building us.

-Jim Rohn, entrepreneur, business philosopher, success coach, and author of more than thirty books, including *Leading an Inspired Life*

38

I've seen a guy in a Darth Vader costume playing bagpipes on a unicycle.

-Caitlin Giddings, *Runner's World* editor on the craziest thing she has seen on a run

39

As you begin changing your thinking, start immediately to change your behavior. Begin to act the part of the person you would like to become. Take action on your behavior. Too many people want to feel, then take action. This never works.

-John Maxwell, in *Developing the Leader Within You 2.0 Workbook*

40

You ran how far? Are you crazy?

-Reaction you get when you tell a non-runner how far you ran in a race—especially if it was marathon

41

For me, running is both exercise and a metaphor. Running day after day, piling up the races, bit by bit I raise the bar, and by clearing each level I elevate myself.

-Haruki Murakami, a writer with bestsellers in Japan as well as internationally, in *What I Talk About When I Talk About Running: A Memoir*

42

While I was running the race today I heard someone clapping constantly. It was my thighs cheering me on.

-Overheard at a 5k run

43

At some point you've got to drop all the excuses in the trash and run. You've got to say, "Yes, there are obstacle. But I'm going to find a way around them or over them, if necessary, and make time for what I really need to do."

-Kevin Nelson in *The Runner's Book of Daily Inspiration*

44

You can get better. Make the decision to do so and take action...again and again. And notice...you are getting better.

  –Randy L. Thurman

45

It's hard to run and feel sorry for yourself at the same time. Also, there are those hours of clear-headedness that follow a long run.

  –Monte Davis, an American professional basketball player.

46

Running has given me the chance to be a saint, to be a hero. Like everyone else, I want to be challenged. I want to find out whether or not I am a coward. I want to see how much effort I can put out...what I can endure...if I measure up. Running allows that.

  –George Sheehan, physician, senior athlete, and author of many great books, in *George Sheehan on Running to Win: How to Achieve the Physical, Mental & Spiritual Victories of Running*

47

Why can't my friend be normal?!?! Why doesn't she just want to go get a margarita like my other friends?

> -My wife's friend, in pain, at mile 1 of a 5K, because my wife had asked that the two of them run the race together as her birthday gift

48

The battles that count aren't the ones for gold medals. The struggles within yourself—the invisible, inevitable battles inside all of us—that's where it's at.

> -Jesse Owens, an African American track and field athlete who won four gold medals in the 1936 summer Olympic games in Berlin, Germany—in front of Hitler

49

Slow runners make fast runners look good.

> -Message printed on back of a runner's shirt

You're welcome.

> -Printed on the front of the same shirt

50

Don't judge your running by your speed.

> –Amby Burfoot, marathoner, author, and all-
> around good guy, in *The Principles of Running*

51

This is the beginning of a new day. You have been given this day to use as you will. You can waste it or use it for good. What you do today is important because you are exchanging a day of your life for it. When tomorrow comes, this day will be gone forever; in its place is something that you've left behind.... Let it be something good.

> –Mac Anderson, a New Zealand cricketer

52

At any given point in time we are the sum total of all our new beginnings.

> –Charles Gaines, writer

> (*And today is when you make a new beginning in your life.*)

53

I want to run every race with a big heart.

> –Ryan Hall, a great American marathon runner

54

Finding a perfect running shoe is the closest thing to real live magic!

-Amanda Furrer, an American rifle shooter who competes in the 50-meter rifle three positions event.

55

I've got 99 problems, but I'm going running to ignore them for an hour.

-Anonymous

56

I run because punching people is frowned upon.

-Message printed on a runner's shirt

57

For every runner who tours the world running marathons, there are thousands who run to hear the leaves and listen to the rain, and look to the day when it is suddenly as easy as a bird in flight.

-George Sheehan, physician, senior athlete, and author of many great books, including *Running & Being: The Total Experience*

58

As a kid I only had one dream, to be an athlete. When I got sick, I was nearly at my heaviest, and it hit me: This isn't my practice life—this is it. I knew I had to change everything.

> –Charlie Jabaley, also known as Charlie Rocket, who, at 300 pounds and diagnosed with a brain tumor, started running and completed the Ironman in 16 hours and 41 minutes

Running can save you!

> –Charlie Jabaley

59

I used to say, "I hope things change." Then I learned that the only way things are going to change for me is when *I* change.

> –Jim Rohn, entrepreneur, business philosopher, success coach, and author of more than thirty books, including *The Power of Ambition*

60

I never go for a run and wish I hadn't.

> –An advertisement for Brooks running gear

> (*Except for that neighborhood 5k when I learned about "the trots."*)

61

The process of [attaining] your own personal goal is a journey that takes longer than one day. [However, it] is the decision to reach your goal that can be done in one day. If you are a person ready for change, today can be your day!

> –Cody Bobay, in *Lose 40 LBS in 1 Day: A 40-Day Journey to Optimal Health*

62

Accept the ups and downs you will experience. You are going to have days you feel like you're flying and days you struggle. This is normal for all runners.

> –Grete Waitz and Gloria Averbuch, in *Run Your First Marathon: Everything You Need to Know to Reach the Finish Line*

63

I run because it's good for me. Also because I like to eat. A lot.

> –Message printed on a runner's shirt

64

The advice I have for beginners is the same philosophy that I have for runners of all levels of experience and ability—consistency, a sane approach, moderation, and making your running an enjoyable, rather than dreaded, part of your life.

–Bill Rogers, in *Lifetime Running Plan*

65

Maybe people—both able bodied and amputees—can look at me and say, "You know what? Life is tough, but if this guy can make it, then I can make it."

–Scott Rigsby, who in 2007 became the first double amputee to complete an Ironman triathlon

66

What I did in those early months wasn't "training." It was more about trying not to get hurt than trying to get better.

> -John Bingham, in *No Need for Speed: A Beginner's Guide to the Joy of Running*

67

Running removes us briefly from the fragmentation and depersonalization of the digital world.

> -Amby Burfoot, marathoner, author, and all-around good guy, in *The Runner's Guide to the Meaning of Life*

68

If you don't like how things are, change it! You're not a tree.

> -Jim Rohn, entrepreneur, business philosopher, success coach, and author of more than thirty books, including *The Keys to Success*

69

Do or do not. There is no try.

> -Yoda

70

Run mad as often as you choose, but do not faint!

—Jane Austen, in *Love and Friendship*

(*Good advice. Fainting, while running, is very bad and can lead to flat nose syndrome.*)

71

Dwell on the beauty of life. Watch the stars and see yourself running with them.

-Marcus Aurelius, Roman emperor from 161 to 180 A.D., in *Meditations*

72

The more you run, the more it will become part of your non-running life. The more you make it part of your non-running life, the more you will run. It's a lovely circle to be caught in.

-Kevin Nelson, in *The Runner's Book of Daily Inspiration: A Year of Motivation, Revelation, and Instruction*

73

You have to want it, you have to plan for it, you have to fit it into a busy day, you have to be mentally tough, you have to use others to help you.

> –Amby Burfoot, marathoner, author, and all-around good guy

74

Look at my watch. Breathe. Keep your head up. Breathe. Repeat. I had one goal: Set a PR.

> –Jessica Hays, entering the final stretch of a 5K. She beat her PR (personal record) by six minutes at 1:04. 2 years earlier, at 34 she weighed 436 pounds. Here she was 36 and weighed 385, a 51 pound weight loss.

75

For so long, I accepted my fate, I thought, "Well I'm obese and I can't do anything." That's not the case at all. I can do it. Slowly, but surely, everything gets a bit easier.

> –Jessica Hays, see previous quote

76

Running complements the work I do in therapy, every mile a reminder that I'm alive and that life is good. And when I need it, running is always there for me.

> –Kate Perelman, a federal contractor and a runner, sharing how running helps fight depression.

77

You don't get the butt you want by sitting on it.

> –Message printed on a runner's shirt

78

You are never given a wish without also being given the power to make it true. You may have to work for it, however.

> –Richard Bach in *Illusions*

79

Running is about finding your inner peace, and so is a life well lived.

> –Dean Karnazes, an American ultramarathon runner

80

Running burns more calories in less time than any other exercise.

-Amby Burfoot, marathoner, author, and all-around good guy, in *The Principles of Running*

81

Running prowess may seem unimportant to an antelope until that rare moment in its life when a lion gives chase.

-Bernd Heinrich, in *Why We Run: A Natural History*

82

What the years have shown me is that running clarifies the thinking process as well as purifies the body. I think best—most broadly and fully—when I am running.

-Amby Burfoot, marathoner, author, and all-around good guy, in *The Runner's Guide to the Meaning of Life*

83

Why do I run? Well, you don't hear about a golfer's high.

-Scott Douglas, author of *Running Is My Therapy: Relieve Stress and Anxiety, Fight Depression, and Live Happier*

84

A good run is like a cup of coffee...I'm much nicer after I've had one.

–Message printed on a runner's shirt.

85

Crossing the starting line may be an act of courage, but crossing the finish line is an act of faith. Faith is what keeps us going when nothing else will. Faith is the emotion that will give you victory over your past, the demons in your soul, and all of those voices that tell you what you can and cannot do and can and cannot be.

–John Bingham, one of the most widely quoted runners and a great writer himself, author of *The Courage to Start: A Guide to Running for Your Life*

86

The world is divided into two kinds of people: runners and non-runners.

–Marc Bloom, in *The Runner's Bible*

87

A slow spiritual death over 30-40 years of tolerating the mediocre.

–Tim Ferris, on what he calls "dying," in *The 4-Hour Workweek: Escape 9-5, Live Anywhere, and Join the New Rich*

88

"What's the world's greatest lie?" the boy asked, completely surprised.

"It's this: that at a certain point in our lives, we lose control of what's happening to us, and our lives become controlled by fate. That's the world's greatest lie."

–Paul Coelho, in *The Alchemist*

89

If your why is strong enough, you'll figure out the how.

–Bill Walsh, Superbowl-winning coach

(*What's your why?*)

90

The Hopis consider running a form of prayer; they offer every step as a sacrifice to a loved one, and in return ask the Great Spirit to match their strength with some of his own.

> –Christopher McDougall, an American author and journalist, in *Born to Run: A Hidden Tribe, Superathletes, and the Greatest Race the World Has Ever Seen*

91

Race entry $60. Running shoes $90. Chafing in places you didn't know chafed, priceless.

> –Sign at a running store

92

You have to want to change more than you want to be the same.

> –Bill Philips, an American entrepreneur and author, in *Body for Life: 12 Weeks to Mental and Physical Strength*

93

I think I can, I think I can, I think I can.

>   -The little engine in *The Little Engine That Could,*
>   by Watty Piper

I think I can, I know I can, I simply have to stay on course
and keep chugging along.

>   -Amby Burfoot, marathoner, author, and all-
>   around good guy, in *The Runner's Guide to the
>   Meaning of Life.*

94

Wake up, say thanks, and go run.

>   –Michael D'Aulerio, author of *A Runner's Secret: One Run Will Get It Done*

95

There's an athlete inside each of us waiting to be released.

>   –Mark Bravo, a writer, broadcaster, and veteran of fifty marathons, in *Momentum: 77 Observations Toward a Life Well Lived*

96

The goal is to be able to run freely and joyfully for the rest of your life, and for you to enjoy the full range of benefits that running offers—physically, mentally...and yes, spiritually.

>   –Danny Dreyer, running coach and ultramarathoner, in *ChiRunning: A Revolutionary Approach to Effortless, Injury-Free Running*

97

How do you best move towards mastery? To put it simply, you practice diligently, but you practice primarily for the sake of practice itself.

>   –George Leonard, in his great book *Mastery: The Keys to Success and Long-Term Fulfillment*

98

You're the slowest runner...so far.

-Sign at a marathon

99

A race is your ultimate accountability partner.

-Randy L. Thurman

100

You run to no one's beat but your own. No one else is making you run. The responsibility for running is yours completely.

-*Runner's World Training Diary*

101

I wasn't thinking of a gold medal. I went out to have fun and a great time.

-Sarah Hughes, 2002 Olympic gold medal winner in women's figure skating

102

The key ingredient, in my opinion, to successful mental training is what I refer to as a "warrior attitude."

–Bob Glover and Shelly-lynn Florence Glover, in *The Competitive Runner's Handbook: The Bestselling Guide to Running 5Ks through Marathons*

103

We learn to walk by stumbling.

–Bulgarian Proverb

104

Pain is temporary, but your finishing time posted on the internet is forever.

–Unknown
(*But if you doubt this, I can still pull up my times from ten years ago.*)

105

Like my shirt? After the race, I'll let you read the front.

–Message printed on the back of a runner's shirt

(*Seen as the wearer goes blazing by.*)

106

Some seek the comfort of their therapist's office, others head to the corner pub and dive into a pint, but I chose running as my therapy.

–Dean Karnazes, who completed 50 marathons in 50 states on 50 consecutive days, author of *Ultramarathon Man: Confessions of an All-Night Runner*

107

The person who starts the race is not the same person who finishes the race.

–Message on a sign at a marathon race

(*The same can be said for anyone who undertakes a worthy endeavor. Go for it!*)

108

What the mind of man can conceive and believe, he can achieve.

–Napoleon Hill, author of the amazing book *Think and Grow Rich*

109

"I can't believe impossible things," said Alice.

"I daresay you haven't much practice," said the Queen. "When I was your age, I always did it for half-an-hour a day. Why, sometimes I've believed as many as six impossible things before breakfast."

> –Alice and the Queen in *Alice's Adventures in Wonderland* by Lewis Carroll
>
> (*And...see next quote.*)

110

Ya gotta believe.

> –New York Mets rallying cry, as heard in August 1973.
>
> (*They were in last place at the time, with just 44 games to go in the season, and ended up first in the National League East.*)

111

Belief creates the actual fact.... The greatest revolution of my generation is the discovery that individuals, by changing their inner attitudes of mind, can change the outer aspects of their lives.

> –William James, Harvard physician and psychologist
>
> (*One of my all-time favorite quotes.*)

112

If you can read this, thanks! I'm not last.

-Message printed on the back of a runner's shirt

113

I frequently tramped eight or ten miles through the deepest snow to keep an appointment with a beech tree.

-Henry David Thoreau, American essayist, poet, and philosopher

(*What's your beech tree?*)

114

The secret to effective, enjoyable envisioning lies in one simple habit: allowing yourself the mental freedom to dream without criticism.

-Dan Clements and Tara Gignac, in *Escape 101: The Four Secrets to Taking a Sabbatical or Career Break Without Losing Your Money*

115

The first thing I had to do was learn that I could do it.

-Sue Stricklin, runner

116

Okay, maybe I should reevaluate how I feel.

> -Randy L. Thurman

> *(After running the last six miles of a marathon to help a friend in the freezing rain and hail, I was feeling awful and very not happy. Then I saw a happy marathoner with blades on both legs—a double amputee—celebrating his achievement.)*

117

Running is a privilege; never take it for granted.

> -Unknown

118

Losing weight is hard. Running is hard. Choose your hard.

> -Unknown

119

People sometimes sneer at those who run every day, claiming they'll go to any length to live longer. But don't think that's the reason most people run. Most runners run not because they want to live longer, but because they want to live life to the fullest. If you're going to while away the years, it's far better to live them with clear goals and fully alive than in a fog, and I believe running helps you to do that. Exerting yourself to the fullest within your individual limits: that's the essence of running, and a metaphor for life—and for me, for writing as well. I believe many runners would agree.

> –Haruki Murakami, a writer with bestsellers in Japan as well as internationally, in *What I Talk About When I Talk About Running*

120

Smile if you're not wearing underwear.

> –Sign at a running event

121

It changed my life enormously. I had my head firmly planted in the sand. Now I see how flimsy life is.

> –Priscilla Welch, who broke records as a marathoner in the 1980s, on her 1992 cancer diagnosis

122

There is nothing so momentary as a sporting achievement, and nothing so lasting as the memory of it.

-Greg Dening, Australian historian of the Pacific islands.

123

Billy, slow down! Are you nuts?

-Charlie Rodgers to Bill Rodgers at the 1975 Boston Marathon

(*Bill Rodgers went on to win.*)

After he won, I vowed never to question him again.

-Charlie Rodgers after Bill Rodgers won the 1975 marathon

(*Beware of those who question what you can do.*)

124

Some days it's not about the speed or the miles. It's just about the therapy.

-Pinterest meme

125

He who is outside the door has already a good part of his journey behind him.

-Dutch proverb

126

There is no finish line...which makes me wish I'd brought toilet paper.

-Unknown

127

If you're running on the treadmill next to me, YES...we are racing!

-A popular Facebook meme

128

My whole teaching in one sentence is, "Run slowly, run daily, drink moderately, and don't eat like a pig."

-Earnest Van Aaken, German physician and running coach

129

Let me win. But if I cannot win, let me be brave in the attempt.

> –Special Olympics athlete oath

130

As the fog and devastation of my crime and incarceration began to lift, I resolved to turn toward hope and make something salvageable of the wreckage that was my life. One foot in front of the other, I started to run toward making myself better. RFA (Running Free Alaska) is a lifesaving resource.

> –Sarah, 41, inmate at Hiland Mountain Correctional Center

131

If it's something you gotta do, you might as well enjoy it.

> –Mike Gundy, Oklahoma State University football coach, quoting his dad, Ray, regarding football practice and life

132

Runner's High. Still legal in all 50 states.

> –Message printed on a runner's shirt

133

Run. Because the zombies will eat the untrained ones first!

-Heather Dakota, in *Zombie Apocalypse Survival Guide*

134

The strength within you is greater than the task ahead of you.

-Ralph Waldo Emerson, American essayist, lecturer, philosopher

135

You can do it! You're a tough dude!

-Randy L. Thurman.

(*My favorite words of encouragement. I say them to myself and others during a trying stretch of a race.*)

136

We must be willing to get rid of the life we've planned, so as to have the life that is waiting for us.

-Joseph Campbell, American author and philosopher

(*I'm not saying it will be easy, I'm saying it will be worth it.*)

137

How would you describe the worst run you ever had? Precious!

-Hal Higdon, American distance runner, author of more than 36 books, including *Marathon: The Ultimate Training Guide*

138

Everything changed the day I understood that if I was to become a runner, I would have to run with the body I had.

> –John Bingham, American distance runner and author, in *The Courage to Start: A Guide to Running for Your Life*

139

Getting more exercise isn't only good for your waistline. It's a natural antidepressant that leaves you in a great mood.

> –Auliq Ice, author, venture capitalist, social investor, humanist, and philanthropist

140

I thought they said Rum!

> –Message printed on a runner's shirt

141

There are few greater joys in life than passing people who went out too fast on the first mile.

> –Randy L. Thurman

142

If you can't run, you crawl. If you can't crawl—you find someone to carry you.

> –Joss Whedon, American producer, director, comic book writer.

143

Always beware of runs that have the phrase in the description, "Gentle, rolling hills."

> –Advice from a seasoned runner when asked which marathon was best to BQ
>
> (*"BQ" refers to qualifying for the Boston Marathon.*)

144

I always tell beginning runners: Train your brain first. It's much more important than your heart or legs.

> –Amby Burfoot, marathoner, author, and all-around good guy, in *The Principles of Running: Practical Lessons from My First 100,000 Miles*

145

Dwell not upon weariness, thy strength shall be according to the measure of thy desire.

> –Arab proverb

146

Desire is want on steroids.

> –Dan Clements and Tara Gignac, in *Escape 101: The Four Secrets to Taking a Sabbatical or Career Break Without Losing Your Money*

147

Let's wake up super early and go run really fast and far.

> –Supposedly from the diary of an insane person

148

During the race people would pass me (or I, them) and say, "You're quite an inspiration." But that works both ways in that it inspires me. After all, when someone calls you an inspiration, what are you going to do, quit?

> –Richard Vaughn, marathoner in a wheelchair

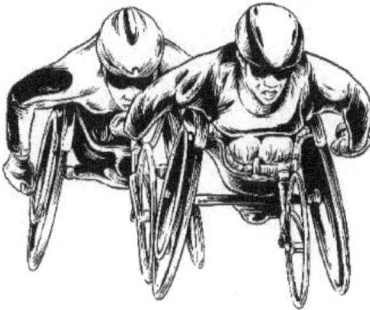

149

When running for exercise and not competition, you should run at an even pace that allows you to talk comfortably. If you run too fast and get breathless, you may not be able to go the distance.

> -*The U.S. Navy Seal Guide to Fitness and Nutrition*

150

Strong reasons make strong actions.

> -William Shakespeare, English playwright and poet

151

What I've learned from running is that the time to push hard is when you're hurting like crazy and you want to give up. Success is often just around the corner.

> -James Dyson, British inventor, industrial designer, and founder of the Dyson company

152

There's nothing quite like the feeling you get from knowing you're in good physical condition. I wake up alert and singing in the morning, ready to go.

> -Stan Gerstein, runner

153

Everyone is an athlete. The only difference is that some of us are in training, and some are not.

-George Sheehan, physician, senior athlete, and author of many great books, including *Running & Being: The Total Experience*

154

Running: Cheaper than therapy.

-Message on a bumper sticker

155

How long should you try? Until.

-Jim Rohn, entrepreneur, business philosopher, success coach, and author of more than thirty books, including *My Philosophy for Successful Living*

156

Every run is a work of art, a drawing on each day's canvas. Some runs are shouts and some runs are whispers. Some runs are eulogies and others celebrations.

-Dagny Scott Barrio, writer, editor, and speaker

157

Life can pull you down, but running always lifts you up.

>   -Jenny Hadfield, marathoner, coach, and author

158

Argue for your limitations and, sure enough, they're yours.

>   -Richard Bach, in *Illusions: The Adventures of a Reluctant Messiah*

159

If you're brave enough to start, you're strong enough to finish.

>   –Gary Ryan Blair, American sports coach

The miracle isn't that I finished, the miracle is that I had the courage to start.

>   -John Bingham, American distance runner and author

160

When adversity strikes, it may be what is needed to be successful.

>   -Sign in a football locker room

>   (*Please note: It says, "When..." not "If...."*)

161

I run because long after my footprints fade away, maybe I will have inspired a few to reject the easy path, hit the trails, put one foot in front of the other, and come to the same conclusion I did: I run because it always takes me where I want to go.

-Dean Karnazes, completed 50 marathons in 50 states on 50 consecutive days, author of *Ultramarathon Man: Confessions of an All-Night Runner*

162

I began running after I became a writer. Since being a writer requires sitting at a desk for hours, I figured that without exercising I'd get out of shape. That was 22 years ago.

-Haruki Murakami, a writer with bestsellers in Japan as well as internationally, in *What I Talk About When I Talk About Running*

163

Except for .001 percent of the running population, everyone's in the exact same position: there will always be people slower than you, and people faster.

-Miles, in his column "Ask Miles" in *Runner's World* magazine

164

What do you want for yourself? Think about that. Make the commitment, then do it. If you can't do it right away, see it, visualize it. The power of the vision pulls you there.

–Randy L. Thurman

165

Running is my private time, my therapy, my religion.

–Gail W. Kislevitz, runner and author

166

Set aside a time solely for running. Running is more fun if you don't have to rush through it.

–Jim Fixx, helped popularize the sport of running by demonstrating its health benefits, author of the classic *The Complete Book of Running*

167

You're not slow. You're just enjoying the course.

–Message on a sign at a running event

168

I knew he was fast, but I never knew how fast until I saw him playing tennis with himself.

-Lou Holtz, American football player and coach, on his player Rocket Ishmail.

(*Now, that's fast!*)

169

Never underestimate the power that one good workout will have on your mind. Keeping the dream alive is half the battle.

-Kara Goucher, American distance runner.

170

If you don't think you were born to run you're not only denying history, you're denying who you are.

-Christopher McDougall, American author and journalist, author of *Born to Run: A Hidden Tribe, Superathletes, and the Greatest Race the World Has Ever Seen*

171

Yes, I am round. Yes, I am slow. Yes, I run as though my legs are tied together at the knees. But I am running. And that is all that matters.

> -John "the Penguin" Bingham, American distance runner and author of *The Courage to Start: A Guide to Running for Your Life*

172

If you want to be wealthy, study wealth. If you want to be happy, study happiness.

> -Jim Rohn, entrepreneur, business philosopher, success coach, and author of more than thirty books, in *How to Have Your Best Year Ever*
>
> (*And with this in mind, it seems reasonable to say, if you want to be the best runner you can be, study running.*)

173

When I go to the Boston Marathon now, I have wet shoulders—women fall into my arms crying. They're weeping for joy because running has changed their lives. They feel they can do anything.

> -Kathrine Switzer, author, television commentator, and the first woman to enter the Boston Marathon

174

If you're not enthusiastic, act as if you are enthusiastic and you'll be enthusiastic.

-Dale Carnegie, American author and lecturer

(*Run enthusiastically. Especially when you don't feel enthusiastic.*)

175

If you want to find the real competition, just look in the mirror. After a while you'll see your rivals scrambling for second place.

-Criss Jami, American poet, essayist, existentialist philosopher, and musician for the band Crymson Gryphon

176

Run often and run long, but never outrun your joy of running.

-Julie Isphording, winner of the 1990 Los Angeles Marathon

177

I could feel my anger dissipating as the miles went by–you can't run and stay mad!

> –Kathrine Switzer, author, television commentator, and the first woman to enter the Boston Marathon

178

They knew him only as another of those crazy runners who goes out every day to punish himself into a state of fitness. And to give the dogs and the motorists fits.

> –Bruce Tuckman, author of *Long Road to Boston*

179

It is not so much that I began to run, but that I continued.

> –Hal Higdon, American distance runner and author of more than 36 books, including *Marathon: The Ultimate Training Guide*

180

You feel good while you're running and you feel even better when you're finished.

> –Fred Lebow, founder of the New York City Marathon

181

My philosophy on running is: I don't dwell on it, I do it.

-Joan Benoit Samuelson, Olympic Gold Medalist

182

Before you criticize someone, you should run a mile in their shoes. That way, when you criticize them, you're a mile away and you have their shoes.

-Unknown

183

We wouldn't be alive without love, we wouldn't have survived without running. Maybe we shouldn't be surprised that getting better at one could make you better at the other.

-Christopher McDougall, American author and journalist, author of *Born to Run: A Hidden Tribe, Superathletes, and the Greatest Race the World Has Ever Seen*

184

Doing something for yourself like running, and using it to test yourself, will only make you feel better about your career or your family role.

> –Joan Benoit Samuelson, first Olympic women's marathon winner, who held the fastest time for an American woman at the Chicago Marathon for 32 years after winning the race in 1985

185

I thought this was a "Law and Order" marathon!

> –Message printed on the back of a runner's shirt

186

One run can change your day. Many runs can change your life.

> –Anonymous

187

A one-hour run is 4% of your day. You have no excuses.

> –Anonymous

188

We all die. Not living is the failure.

-Sidney J. Winawer, physician

189

This is a 5k, right?

-Message printed on the shirt of a runner at a
marathon

190

In running you're successful just by doing it. You learn
how far you can take yourself and how to compete within
yourself. When you do that, you start feeling good about
yourself.

-Sue Stricklin, runner

191

Perseverance is not a long race; it is many short races one
after another.

-Walter Elliott, author

192

Run as if a hand just reached out and grabbed you!

-Message on a sign at a running event

193

Don't take yourself so seriously! Runners tend to get so caught up in time goals, training regimens, and racking up the miles that we can forget to stop and smell the roses. Or, you know, explore the world's great corn mazes.

> -Denise Malan, author, in *The Runner's Bucket List,* just before her description of the Corn Maze 5k run in Spring Grove, Illinois, which has 250 turns—and incredibly, the course changes every year

194

Someone called me a freak of nature once for what I do. I don't know if that's true or not, but there aren't many people who are 99, still living, and not many running a mile.

> -George Etzweiler, age 99, who has run the Mount Washington road race, with 7.43 miles and a 5,000-foot ascent, 13 times

195

When dad died, running was a release for me. I tend to store things inside me, and it's only when I go out for a run that I get it all out.

> -Steve Jones, British rock guitarist, singer, and actor

196

Run in the morning...before your brain figures out what you're doing.

-Anonymous

197

"I breathe in strength and breathe out weakness" is my mantra during marathons—it calms me down and helps my focus.

-Amy Hastings, an Irish actress who has worked in film, television, and theatre

198

I traveled the whole world looking for adventure and found it in my own body.

-Unknown

199

Do you not know that your bodies are temples of the Holy Spirit, who is in you?

-1 Corinthians 6:19

200

Your body is the temple of the soul.

> -Jan Hutchins, American TV and radio journalist, producer, and media consultant

201

There is no self-mastery without discipline. And there is no greater source of discipline than the effort demanded in overcoming obstacles.

> -Simone Weil, French mystic, social philosopher, activist, and author

202

All we are given is possibilities—to make ourselves one thing or another.

> -José Ortega y Gasset, Spanish philosopher

203

Running is alone time that lets my brain unspool the tangles that build up over days...I run, pound it out on the pavement, channel that energy into my legs, and when I'm done with my run, I'm done with it.

> -Rob Haneisen, runner

204

We must recognize that our real duty is always found in running in the direction of our worthiest desires.

-Randolph Bourne, American journalist, social critic, and political activist

205

Quitting never feels as good as finishing.

-New Balance advertisement

206

I'm just doing what I love to do—swimming, biking, running—whether I have legs or not. If I had legs, I might not be as active.

-Rudy Garcia-Tolson, who has run a mile in less than six minutes on two prosthetic legs.

207

Run with passion!

-Houston Marathon advertisement

208

I'm not interested in athletics, I'm only interested in achievement. Fix your goals and work for them.

> –Percy Cerutty, Australian coach, to runner Herb Elliott, who later set the world record in the mile.

209

I'm not a runner.

> (*Then she ran in a Color Run, got hooked on running, built up to a marathon, and made it through a host of challenges of running and life.*)

I've wanted to give up a hundred times.... I kept going. I achieved more than I ever imagined. And now I know: I can do things that seem impossible. I can always keep moving forward—no matter what's going on around me or within me, no matter who is or isn't at my side. I can run through anything.

> –Denise Murphy Drespling, in her essay "Through Anything" in *Chicken Soup for the Soul: Running for Good*

210

Just when you think you can't run another step...suck it up! Because you're four miles away from home and that's where the food is.

-Unknown

211

The road is a good listener.

-Message on a poster for runners

212

Running is a way of life for me, just like brushing my teeth. If I don't run for a few days, I feel as if something's been stolen from me.

-John A. Kelley, a two-time Olympian who ran in the Boston Marathon a record 61 times and was champion twice

213

Find a thought to serve you better.

(*What a great thought!*)

When the going gets tough, gratitude keeps you going.

-Matthew Meyer, Boston marathoner and running coach

214

I think I get addicted to the feelings associated with the end of a long run. I love feeling empty, clean, worn out, and sweat-purged. I love that good ache of the muscles that have done me proud.

–Kristin Armstrong, author of *Mile Markers: The 26.2 Most Important Reasons Why Women Run*

215

Psychologists will tell you that positive thoughts lead to positive emotions, and that often leads to positive outcomes. I often tell my athletes to practice having a positive mantra during long runs.

–Janet Hamilton, owner of Running Strong, an online coaching service based in Atlanta, Georgia

216

When I started running, I started dreaming. It couldn't be helped. The mind works as hard as the body does during exercise.

–Bart Yasso, an inductee in the Running USA Hall of Champions who has run races on all seven continents, known as the "mayor of running"

217

Age is a case of mind over matter. If you don't mind, it doesn't matter.

-Satchel Paige, major league pitcher who pitched his last game at the age of 59

218

Not feeling like your long run today? Been there, done that. What helps me is to not think about the long run, just think about running a mile. More often than not, after a mile I'm ready to do the rest.

-Randy L. Thurman

219

We don't know what you're doing, but keep doing it.

-Cancer doctors to Scott Spitz, who mystified the doctors with his improved medical condition, believed to be attributable to his running.

Cancer is trying to kill me, but it's going to have to catch me first.

-Scott Spitz in *Runner's World* magazine

220

On your good days, run hard. On your bad days, run as long as you need to.

–Unknown

221

If you want to change your body, exercise. If you want to change your life, become a runner.

–Unknown

222

Every time I run, I say CF won't stop me.

–Sabrina Walker, who when diagnosed with cystic fibrosis at age 4 was given a life expectancy of age 8, and who is now 34 years old and newly married with a life expectancy of 38.

223

It's just as important to remember that each footstrike carries you forward, not backward. And every time you put on your running shoes you are different in some way than you were the day before. This is all good news.

–John Bingham, American distance runner and author, in *Runner's World* magazine

224

You think you're tired? We stayed up all night making these signs.

–Message on a sign at Laugh-and-a-Half-Marathon

(*The creator of the sign was sleeping in a blow-up bed next to the sign.*)

225

In running it is man against himself, the cruelest of opponents. The other runners are not the real enemies. His adversary lies within him, in his ability with brain and heart to master himself and his emotions.

–Glenn Cunningham, who in his childhood was severely burned, almost losing his legs, and went on to become one of America's greatest milers.

226

If I can get better, why not?

–Emil Zatopek, a distance runner best known for winning three gold medals at the 1952 Summer Olympics in Helsinki.

227

When I finished I blew kisses and high fived everyone! Running has made a world of difference to me. I feel so accomplished.

> –Jimmy Jenson, the first person with Down Syndrome to officially run the New York City Marathon

228

Clear your mind of can't.

> –Samuel Johnson, English poet, biographer, essayist, lexicographer

229

More than one laughed when I said I was going to run a marathon. But man, the feeling I had when that starting gun went off, and when I crossed the finish line—WOW!

> –Randy L. Thurman

230

I look inside and don't see wrinkles or a tired heart, I see an unspent youth.

> –Ralph Waldo Emerson, American essayist, lecturer, philosopher, at the age of 62

231

It's the ones who make fun of me, they get me to the finish line.

> –John Young, who at 4' 4" has to take about 24,000 extra steps more than the average runner to finish a marathon, and who ran—and finished—the Boston Marathon.

232

There is nothing hard about running the hundred miles a week I do. Almost anyone can do it. The hard part is making yourself roll out of bed in the morning and start running.

> –George Young, the only American to run in four Olympic games

233

There's a recovering heroin addict running the marathon. Maybe I can do it.

> –Someone watching Chris Herren, a recovering heroin addict, run a marathon

> (*Or so he hopes.*)

234

Courage overrides self-doubt but does not end it.

> –Mason Cooley, an American aphorist known for
> his witty aphorisms

235

I need to prove an 83-year-old can still compete. Boston
is a magical course. I'm sure God will be next to me
enjoying it as well.

> –Sister Madonna Buder, 83, after being asked what
> it takes to be the oldest woman to run the Boston
> Marathon.

236

Long may you run.

> –An often-shared message of inspiration among
> runners.

237

Running is about changing lives. Most of us feel significant
or powerful through running, and people who have never
had a sense of it suddenly gain it.

> –Kathrine Switzer, author, television commentator,
> and the first woman to enter the Boston
> Marathon, spoken before women were allowed to
> run in it

238

Why do you run circles around your house? Because you can't end at 5.95.

-Just ask any runner.

239

The bond that links your true family is not one of blood, but of respect and joy in each other's life. Rarely do members of one family grow up under the same roof.

-Richard Bach, in *Illusions: The Adventures of a Reluctant Messiah*

(*If you're a runner, you're a member of a running family. Careful, it's a tight knit group.*)

240

Life gives you a choice...either learn to overcome challenges or succumb to them.

-Bill Phillips, in *Body for Life: 12 Weeks to Mental and Physical Strength*

241

I had mixed emotions. The camera on the home straight filmed me crossing the line 5 seconds *after* a guy dressed as a toilet finished.

>   –Brandon Taylo, marathon runner, when asked how it felt to finish the marathon.

242

You've got a look. It says, "Catch me if you can."

>   –Garman advertisement

243

Away from cars.

>   –Joshua Carlos, a runner and assistant running coach, when asked, "Where do you run?"

244

Live not as though there were a thousand years ahead of you. Fate is at your elbow; make yourself good while life and power are still yours.

>   –Marcus Aurelius, Roman emperor and philosopher who wrote *Meditations* around 175 AD

245

Run like you're chasing squirrels!

> –Message on a sign at a running event, with a big picture of a dog

246

I have heard a million people say that running is the most boring activity that they can possibly imagine. Since I'm sure I'm not any smarter or wittier than these people, I can only guess that they never learned to listen as they run. If they did, they would surely be entertained and informed by their own thoughts.

> –Amby Burfoot, marathoner, author, and all-around good guy, in *The Runner's Guide to the Meaning of Life*

247

You miss every shot you don't take.

> –Wayne Gretzky, all-time great hockey player who holds the record for most career regular-season goals

248

If you add a little to a little, and then do it again, soon that little shall be much.

> –Hesiod, Greek poet

249

When I started running, I hoped it would make me healthier. It did that. And so much more.

> –Phil Cruz, who started training for a marathon after being diagnosed with incurable cancer, and who is still volunteering as a coach three years after his diagnosis

250

As my life was getting pieced back together, running gave me direction.

> –Jillian Campregher, who, after two DUI's and 40 days in jail followed by unemployment and severe depression, began taking long walks to clear her head and eventually started running.

251

Beware of falling cows.

> –Message on a sign next to a cliff
>
> (*This has to be the #1 road sign runners don't want to see.*)

252

I'm just trying to cross the street!

> –Message on a sign at a running event

253

Running: Cheaper than plastic surgery!

-Message printed on a runner's shirt

254

No matter how big and inactive you are, no matter how longstanding your hatred of running or exercise of any kind, if you give it a try and stick to it, the day will come when it no longer sucks—when life no longer sucks...the day will come when you want to live forever.

-Marc Parent, in his column *Newbie Chronicles* in *Runner's World* magazine

255

Lead poisoning.

-Al Richmond, age 75, describing being shot three times by a mugger

(*Six months after the shooting, he ran the Marine Corp Marathon at 4:40.*)

256

I'll be damned—if that old fart can do it, so can I.

-A young Lieutenant Colonel after having run ten miles and in need of inspiration, referring to 75-year-old Al Richmond

257

A strong butt is the key to a happy life.

> -Jordan Metzl, physician, in his explanation of why weak glutes makes runners more prone to injury

258

Fitness takes time.... Push too hard, too soon, and you'll be discouraged

> -Greg McMillan, a running coach who advises newbies as well as Olympic qualifiers

259

If you really want to do something, you'll find a way. If you don't, you'll find an excuse.

> -Jim Rohn, entrepreneur, business philosopher, success coach, and author of more than thirty books, including *Leading an Inspired Life*

260

You could have chosen chess!

> -Message on a sign at a running event

261

When I stand before God at the end of my life, I would hope that I would not have a single bit of talent left, and could say, "I used everything you gave me!"

> –Erma Bombeck, an American humorist who achieved great popularity as a syndicated columnist who shared her take on suburban home life from the mid-1960s until the late 1990s

262

Don't try to be perfect; just be an excellent example of being human.

> –Anthony Robbins, life and business strategist, coach, motivational speaker, and author of *Awaken the Giant Within: How to Take Immediate Control of Your Mental, Emotional, Physical and Financial Destiny!*

263

Faith is taking the first step even when you don't see the staircase.

> –Martin Luther King, Jr., American Christian minister and activist who became the most visible spokesperson and leader in the civil rights movement from 1955 until his assassination in 1968

264

Chance favors those in motion.

> –James H. Austin, an English professional
> footballer who plays as a defender for the Premier
> League team Sheffield United.

265

If you can deal with cancer, you can deal with anything.

> –Gabriel Grunewald, her mantra. Diagnosed with
> cancer at age 22, then at 24 competes for Brooks
> running and went on to run a 1500 in 4:01.

266

Worst parade EVER!

> –Sign at a racing event

267

When nothing seems to help, I go and look at a stone-
cutter hammering away at his rock, perhaps a hundred
times without as much as a crack showing in it. Yet, at the
hundred and first blow it will split it in two, and I know it
is not that last blow that did it, but all
that had come before.

> –Jacob A. Riis, a Danish-American so-
> cial reformer, "muckraking" journalist
> and social documentary photographer.

268

Don't be afraid to go out on a limb. That's where all the fruit is.

-H. Jackson Brown, author of the great *21 Suggestions for Success*

269

Running is a way to help yourself and to achieve the things you want. That's hardly trivial.

-Kevin Nelson in his book *The Runner's Book of Daily Inspiration*

270

I love to run. This is just part of my life. It's the way I live.

-Johnny Kelley, perennial Boston Marathoner

271

Finish strong. It's the only respectable way to finish.

-Gary Ryan Blair, the head coach of the Texas A&M Aggies women's basketball team.

272

Some people meditate, I run.

-Satcha Pretto, a Honduran Emmy Award winning journalist.

273

Don't Stop! People are Watching!

>   –Sign at a racing event

274

Don't wait. Run while you feel like it, in the way you should. Do it on the track or on the street. Sprint or jog or combine the two. Race the clock or race an imaginary opponent or try to finish a distance you've set for yourself. Do whatever you want, but do it.

>   –Runner's World Training Dairy

275

Just do it.

>   –Nike slogan

276

The people at Nike might say, "Just do it." And I don't think I can say it better. There's such power in action, such excitement, such reward.

>   –Amby Burfoot in his book *The Runner's Guide to the Meaning of Life*

277

Every run presents a new adventure, full of great gifts. We don't have to "win to receive them"—but we have to get out the door.

> –Amby Burfoot sharing lessons the stuck with him on his 50th anniversary of his Boston Marathon

278

The beginner holds the seed of all that is to follow.

> –I Ching

> (*But ya gotta begin.*)

279

We all have two choices when faced with adversity: give up or be great.

> –Amby Palmiero, who, following a below the knee amputation went on to hold world records including the Ironman triathlon

280

If I didn't run, I'd feel like you do.

> –Bumper sticker

281

Ever tried. Ever failed. No Matter. Try again. Fail again. Fail better.

> –Samuel Beckett, an Irish novelist, playwright, short story writer, theatre director, poet, and literary translator.

282

Endorphins. The runner's drug of choice.

> –Message printed on a runner's shirt (although, I feel, ibuprofen is probably a close second)

283

Running was exciting, and the more I ran the better I got. It was a fun time and all so new.

> –Priscilla Welch, a British retired marathon runner.

284

I'm only doing this so I can post a picture on Facebook.

> –Message printed on a runner's shirt

285

It does not matter how slowly you go so long as you do not stop.

-Confucius, a Chinese teacher and philosopher

286

AARP member...but ahead of you!

-Message printed on the back of a runner's shirt

287

He thinks he'll be happier in the long run.

-Frank Litsky on Carl Lewis's decision to go to the 800 meters instead of the 100

288

Someone who is busier than you is running right now.

-Nike Ad

289

I view life as a series of training events building up to the big race and final finish line and I am always in training, always in the process of reaching the final goal.

-Matthew Shaffer, ultramarathoner

290

He runs like a man who's just been stabbed in the heart.

-Coach of Emil Zatopek's running style, arguably one of the all-time great runners

291

One person's grinding gait is another's graceful dance. To each their own. To thine own's sole be true.

-Bob Schwartz in his book: *I Run, Therefore I am Nuts!*

292

The marathon is too far and too fickle to be tamed by your intentions.

-Peter Bromka. Marathoner, writer about running.

(*Kind of like life, yes?*)

293

Far better it is to dare mighty things than to rank with those who neither enjoy nor suffer much.

-Theodore Roosevelt, the 26th president of the United States.

294

Not unless they have Dutch Elm disease.

-Rob de Castello, marathoner when asked if it was a problem that his legs looked like tree trunks.

295

Go get 'em. When life gets tough and the path uncertain for everyone:

1. Realized you will survive

2. Realize you will grow from it

3. Take one step forward; breathe, think and unleash the survivor inside.

-Mark Bravo from his book, *Momentum* after having a hip surgery in 2007. He's still running today.

296

I've yet to meet a runner who's happy about slowing down. I know I'm not. But the alternative—quitting is far worse.

-Amby Burfoot sharing lessons that stuck with him

297

Faster! Go faster!

> –Children with various disabilities being pushed in strollers by volunteers at the Eagle Mountain Utah 5k.

298

I just knew...when I heard myself say I "only" ran 6 miles...that I was no slacker.

> –Overheard at the Oklahoma City Marathon

299

You get hooked on morning running. I get to the office and people are half asleep and they ask me, "What are you on?"

> –John Honerkamp, running coach

300

The trick is growing up without growing old.

> –Casey Stengel managing a pro baseball team at the age of 75

301

Don't think of it as getting older!

> –Message on the front of a birthday card

Think of it as getting closer to a realistic BQ time!

> –Message inside the card
>
> (*"BQ" refers to qualifying for the Boston Marathon.*)

302

Running is a gift.

> –Unknown
>
> (*Should be every runner's mantra.*)

303

When you come down to it, what running does is give you the basic skill to live well.

> –George Sheehan, physician, senior athlete, and author of many great books, in George Sheehan on Running to Win: How to Achieve the Physical, Mental & Spiritual Victories of Running

304

I love night runs. I run fast as if someone's chasing me where a hand is reaching out of the ground to grab my ankles.

-Sydney Leroux, pro soccer player

305

Don't fear moving slowly forward...fear standing still.

-Kathleen Harris, an American politician

306

I believe, with all my heart, we are all different and we have the ability to rise above roadblocks that seem impenetrable. We possess, or can develop, characteristics in certain areas that allow us to raise our game and beat the odds.

-Mark Bravo, in *Momentum: 77 Observations Toward a Life Well Lived*

307

I have a mind set of "Just do it." Just do it. If you take the time to think, to make excuses, it doesn't happen. Just do it.

-Larissa Rivers, marketing executive and mother of three, when asked how she gets up early to run

308

When you said friends with benefits, I assumed you owned a running store.

–Message on a sign at a race

309

I expected running would make me feel fitter, healthier and stronger, but what I didn't expect was a new group of fantastic friends.

–Deborah Jones, a runner who said her running pals had become an extended family

310

Gratitude unlocks all you can be.

–Melody Beattie, an American author of self-help books on codependent relationships

311

There seems to be a door on the way to remarkable success that can be passed through only by those willing to persevere beyond the point where the majority stops and turns back.

–Earl Nightingale, author of *The Strangest Secret*

312

We run to undo the damage we've done to body and spirit. We run to find some path of ourselves yet undiscovered.

> –John Bingham, one of the most widely quoted runners and a great writer himself, in *The Courage to Start: A Guide to Running for Your Life*

313

The most important person to stand up to is yourself.

> –Bill Phillips, author of *Body for Life: 12 Weeks to Mental and Physical Strength*

314

A short run is better than no run.

> –Unknown

315

This is a lot of work for a free banana.

> –Message on a sign at a race

316

I believe no human is limited.

> –Eliud Kipchoge, world's fastest marathon runner, first to break the two-hour limit

317

Dead last is better than did not finish, which is better than did not start.

> –Anonymous

318

Every day that I run, I've won over my bad side, the side that says, "Skip it."

> –Chris Herron, motivational speaker and former NBA player who overcame a heroin addiction

319

I didn't feel like running today. Which is exactly why I went.

> –Unknown

320

The runners may push the kids with their legs, but it's the kid's heart that carries everyone across the finish line.

> –Runner Angela Green, volunteer who pushed a child with disabilities in a stroller, in a 5K race.

321

Failure is not fatal, but failure to change might be.

> –John Wooden, all-time great basketball coach who has won more Division1 championships than any other coach

322

There are many challenges to long-distance running, but one of the greatest is the question of where to put one's house keys.

> –Gabrielle Zevin, an American author and screenwriter

323

The more I train, the more I realize I have more speed in me.

> –Leroy Burrell, 1992 Olympic Gold Medalist

324

You can become addicted to the feeling of running, and why not feel good? Why not continue this journey?

-Chris Herron, motivational speaker and former NBA player who overcame a heroin addiction

325

The pursuit of excellence is not a goal; it's a habit.

-Booker T. Washington, an American educator, author, orator, and adviser to multiple presidents of the United States.

326

Go as long as you can, and then take another step.

-Unknown

327

Concentrate on small segments of your race at a time. For example, rather than obsessing about the distance that remains, simply complete the next mile in good form...try another, then another, until the race is done.

-Jerry Lynch, an American professional baseball outfielder and pinch hitter

328

The answer to the big questions in running is the same as the answer to the big questions in life: do the best with what you've got.

-Unknown

329

A year from now you will wish you had started today.

-Karen Lamb, an American character actress and producer

330

Whether a mile or a marathon, you get there the same way...one step at a time. Such is life.

-Baylor Barbee, a best-selling author, award-winning speaker, triathlete, and host of the popular podcast *Shark Theory*

331

Life can pull you down, but running always lifts you up.

-Jenny Hadfield, running coach

332

A runner is real when she takes the first step.

> –Clarissa Pinkola Estés, a first-generation American writer and Jungian psychoanalyst, author of *Women Who Run with the Wolves: Myths and Stories of the Wild Woman Archetype*

333

Workouts are like brushing my teeth; I don't think about them, I just do them. The decision has already been made.

> –Patti Sue Plumer, an American former middle-distance and long-distance runner.

334

Running helps me stay sane and helps me not dwell on worst case scenarios like being paralyzed. It takes a lot of focus to get through races, as my legs have no feeling.

> –Kayla Montgomery, state cross-country champion with multiple sclerosis

335

Instead of sitting here feeling sorry for myself, I set a goal and show people on dialysis that it is not the end of the world. You can have a good quality of life.

> –Greg Soderlund, age 66, who lost his kidneys to cancer and runs 30 to 45 miles a week

336

Runner's logic: I'm tired. Let me go for a run.

> –Message printed on a runner's shirt

337

Being defeated is often a temporary condition. Giving up is what makes it permanent.

> –Marilyn vos Savant, an American magazine columnist, author, lecturer, and playwright

338

A runner who avoids injury leaves the competition behind.

> –Unknown

339

Why run? No halftimes. No timeouts. No substitutions. Because humans are born to run.

> –Pablo Escargega, a runner and writer, when asked, "Why run?"
>
> (*He went on to list many more reasons.*)

340

I finished.

> –Larry Gosney, All-American football player at Oklahoma State University when, after completing a marathon, he was asked, "What was your time?"

341

Never, ever, ever judge a run by its first mile.

> –Unknown

342

Always find time for things that make you feel happy to be alive. Go run.

> –Unknown

343

Running won't solve all your problems. But then again, neither will housework.

–Unknown

344

You can count on running: it won't disappoint. If you work at it, if you discipline yourself to run while continuing to enjoy it and have fun, you'll become a stronger and faster runner. You will accomplish things. The rewards will be clear.

–Kevin Nelson, in *The Runner's Book of Daily Inspiration: A Year of Motivation, Revelation, and Instruction*

345

Running should be a relief from stress, a way to help you cope with it, not another stress.

–Bob Glover, runner

346

I'm not trying to be skinny. I'm not trying to be perfect. I'm trying to be strong. I'm trying to be a motivator both to others and to myself. I'm trying to show others that finding something you love as much as I love running can change you.

> –Melissa Edmondson, who is now training for her 9th half-marathon; from *Chicken Soup for the Soul: Running for Good: 101 Stories for Runners & Walkers to Get You Moving* by Amy Newmark and Dean Karnazes

347

Do it for the "Holy S*&$!, you got hot!"

> –Facebook meme and now the title of a weight-loss journal

348

Runners don't do drugs, they make their own...naturally.

> –E. Neil Culbertson, minister, theologian, founder of the Guam Running club, and author of *The Great Northwest Runner's Training Log: 52-Week Edition*

349

The faster you run, the faster you're done.

> –Steve Tiefenthaler, a runner who apparently never heard that the slowest runners get the most for their entry fees

350

Do you believe you can or can't? You're right either way.

> –Henry Ford, paraphrased

351

Running is my Zen moment. I'm alone. I breath deep, zone out, and keep moving. I'm better the rest of the day because of this.

> –Randy L. Thurman, collector of running quotes

352

The marathon is one of those experiences that people tell me allows them the confidence to be able to do a lot of other things in their life that they thought they could never do.

> –Jeff Galloway, an American Olympian and the author of *Galloway's Book on Running*

353

The quality of a person's life is in direct proportion to their commitment to excellence, regardless of their chosen field of endeavor.

-Vince Lombardi, coach of two Super Bowl champion teams and arguably the greatest pro football coach ever

354

Running is quality time...with me.

-Unknown

355

The ultimate goal is to be better today than yesterday, with a plan to become even better tomorrow.

-Amy Rees Anderson, entrepreneur, writer for *Forbes* magazine, and author of *What AWESOME Looks Like: How to Excel in Business and Life*

356

Start now! Don't wonder later, "What if..." and "If only...."

-Unknown

357

A scientific examination of my running would reveal simple maxims: Don't run when your fever is above 101 degrees, and don't try to run long the morning after dinner at an all-you-can-eat salad bar.

-Bob Schwartz, in *I Run Therefore I Am—Nuts!*

358

People always ask me if success is going to change me, and I tell them I sure hope so.

-Randy "Tex" Cobb, heavyweight boxer

359

You have been assigned this mountain so that you can show others it can be moved.

-Mel Robbins, in *The 5-Second Rule: Transform Your Life, Work and Confidence with Everyday Courage*

360

Courage doesn't always roar. Sometimes courage is that little voice at the end of the day that says I'll try again tomorrow.

-Mary Anne Radmacher, author of *Lean Forward into Your Life: Listen Hard, Live with Intention, and Play with Abandon*

361

I just ran 5 miles! What a great workout! I thought that the ice cream truck would never stop.

–Unknown

362

We runners are all a little nutty, but we're good people who just want to enjoy our healthy, primitive challenge. Others may not understand running, but we do, and we cherish it. That's our only message.

–John J. Kelley, winner of the 1957 Boston Marathon and the marathon at the 1959 Pan American Games, and a member of two United States Olympic Marathon teams

363

Struggling and suffering are the essence of a life worth living. If you're not pushing yourself beyond the comfort zone, if you're not demanding more from yourself—expanding and learning as you go—you're choosing a numb existence. You're denying yourself an extraordinary trip.

> –Dean Karnazes, who completed 50 marathons in 50 states on 50 consecutive days, author of Ultramarathon Man: Confessions of an All-Night Runner

364

Cross country running wouldn't be so bad if you lived in a small country.

> –Overheard at a 5K race

365

My life is a gift to me from the Creator. What I do with my life is my gift back to my Creator.

> –Billy Mills, Olympic Gold medalist in 1964 in the 10K

366

We all know that if you run, you are pretty much choosing a life of success because of it.

> –Deena Kastor, bronze medalist in the women's marathon at the 2004 Olympics

367

You are truly your own hero in running. It is up to you to have the responsibility and self-discipline to get the job done.

–Adam Goucher, a retired American cross-country and track and field athlete

368

A run begins the moment you forget you're running.

–Advertisement for Adidas running gear

369

I have found joy, but most of all, I found myself.

–Rene Jordan, who started running at age 45, ran a 5K and won her age group, and was then hooked on running and "became a new person"; from *Chicken Soup for the Soul: Running for Good: 101 Stories for Runners & Walkers to Get You Moving* by Amy Newmark and Dean Karnazes

370

Well, I won't say I can or I can't; but if I do, I do it before most people get up in the morning.

–Bear Bryant, American college football coach and winner of six national championships, when asked if he can walk on water

(*Sounds like a runner, doesn't he?*)

371

And so in my sophomore year I went out for track, because track was the sport where you were least likely to have something thrown at you or have somebody run into you at high speed.

> –Dave Berry, an American author and columnist who wrote a nationally syndicated humor column for the Miami Herald from 1983 to 2005

372

Type out your five favorite quotations and place them where you can see them every day.

> –H. Jackson Browne, author of *Life's Instruction for Wisdom, Success, and Happiness*
>
> (*Or you can tear out pages from your favorite quotebook.*)

373

The marvelous richness of human experience would lose something of rewarding joy if there were no limitations to overcome. The hilltop hour would not be half so wonderful if there were no dark valleys to traverse.

> –Helen Keller, American author, political activist, and lecturer who was deaf and blind from the age of 19 months.

374

Running! If there's any activity happier, more exhilarating, more nourishing to the imagination, I can't think of what it might be. In running the mind flees with the body, the mysterious efflorescence of language seems to pulse in the brain, in rhythm with our feet and the swinging of our arms.

-Joyce Carol Oates, American writer, author of *The Handmaid's Tale*

375

No man who is occupied in doing a very difficult thing, and doing it very well, ever loses his self-respect.

-George Bernard Shaw, an Irish playwright, critic, polemicist, and political activist.

376

If you go to Starbucks more often to use the restroom than to buy coffee, you might be a runner.

-Unknown

377

I don't think about the miles that are coming down the road, I don't think about the mile I'm on right now, I don't think about the miles I've already covered. I think about what I'm doing right now, just being lost in the moment.

> -Ryan Hall, U.S Olympic marathoner, on running a marathon

378

If you have more running clothes than regular clothes in your laundry pile, you might be a runner.

> -Unknown

379

The thirst you feel in your throat and lungs will be gone minutes after the race is over, the pain in your legs within days, but the glory of your finish will last forever.

> -Unknown

380

Frustration is the first step toward improvement. I have no incentive to improve if I'm content with what I can do and if I'm completely satisfied with my pace, distance, and form as a runner. It's only when I face frustration and use it to fuel my dedication that I feel myself moving forward.

> –John Bingham, one of the most widely quoted runners and a great writer himself, author of *The Courage to Start: A Guide to Running for Your Life*

381

The man who moves a mountain begins by carrying away small stones.

> –Confucius, the sixth century B.C. philosopher who emphasized personal and governmental morality, correctness of social relationships, justice, kindness, and sincerity

382

After all, if you run far enough, no one can catch you.

> –V.E. Schwab, American writer

383

Don't bother just to be better than your contemporaries or predecessors. Try to be better than yourself.

-William Faulkner, an American writer and Nobel Prize laureate from Oxford, Mississippi, and one of only four authors to be awarded the Pulitzer Prize for fiction more than once

384

You would run much slower if you were dragging something behind you, like a knapsack or a sheriff.

-Lemony Snicket, fictional character in books by Daniel Handler

385

If you know what an iliotibial band is and where it is located, you might be a runner.

–Randy L. Thurman, collector of running quotes

386

That's the thing about running: your greatest runs are rarely measured by racing success. They are moments in time when running allows you to see how wonderful your life is.

–Kara Goucher, the 10,000 meter silver medalist at the 2007 World Athletics Championships, and a competitor at the 2008 Beijing Olympics and 2012 London Olympics

387

Every step is one less step to take.

–Message on a sign at a half marathon

388

Aim high, but respect the process.

–Amby Burfoot, marathoner, author, and all-around good guy, on the 50th anniversary of his Boston Marathon win

389

FINISH!

–Message on a sign a mile before the finish line

(*One of my favorites!*)

390

Runners are more concerned about rotating our inordinate supply of running shoes than rotating the car tires, we own more waterproof running suits than business suits, and half of our wardrobe has reflective fabric for visibility in the dark.

–Bob Schwartz in his book: *I Run, Therefore I Am—Nuts!*

391

As every runner knows, running is about more than just putting one foot in front of the other; it is about our lifestyle and who we are.

> –Joan Benoit Samuelson, the first women's Olympic Games marathon champion, who won the gold medal at the 1984 Summer Olympics in Los Angeles.

392

All walls have doors.

> –Message on a sign at mile 22 of a marathon, where many runners "hit the wall"

393

What is success? I see success as a journey and I define it, for me, this way: Success is constant and never-ending improvement in the six areas of life: personal, professional, physical, family, financial and spiritual.

> –Randy L. Thurman

394

To be alive, to be able to see, to walk, to have a home, music, paintings, friends—it's all a miracle. I have adapted the technique of living life from miracle to miracle.

> -Arthur Rubinstein, Polish American classical pianist
>
> (*...or to run! It's a miracle, too.*)

395

What is success? Success is nothing more than a few simple disciplines practiced every day.

> -Jim Rohn, entrepreneur, business philosopher, success coach, and author of more than thirty books, including *Leading an Inspired Life*

396

I want my children to understand pushing the envelope and not selling yourself short.

> -Amy Palmiero-Winters, first female amputee to finish the Badwater Ultramarathon, a 135-mile race from Death Valley to Mount Whitney; from the book *Runspirations: Amazing Stories, Timeless Wisdom, and Motivational Quotes to Help You Run Stronger Every Day*, by Amby Burfoot and Gail Waesche Kislevitz

397

Running is my meditation, mind flush, cosmic telephone, mood elevator, and spiritual communion.

-Lorraine Moller, a former athlete from New Zealand who competed in track and later specialized in the marathon

398

It's very hard in the beginning to understand that the whole idea is not to beat the other runners. Eventually you learn that the competition is against the little voice inside you that wants you to quit.

-George Sheehan, physician, senior athlete, and author of many great books, including *Running & Being: The Total Experience*

399

I'm the fast girl your mother warned you about.

-Message printed on a runner's shirt

400

My therapist is the pavement. My drug is endorphins. My foe is the next hill. I am a runner.

-Message printed on a runner's shirt

401

Some runners judge performance by whether they won or lost. Others define success or failure by how fast they ran. Only you can judge your performance. Avoid letting others sit in judgement of you.

> –Hal Higdon, American distance runner, author of more than 36 books, including *Marathon: The Ultimate Training Guide*

402

Running is a road to self-awareness and reliance—you can push yourself to extremes and learn the harsh reality of your physical and mental limitations or coast quietly down a solitary path watching the earth spin beneath your feet.

> –Doris Brown Heritage, American middle- and long-distance runner

403

Invest your time, don't just spend it.

> –Bill Phillips, in Body for Life: 12 Weeks to Mental and Physical Strength

404

I run with my head, my heart and my guts, because physically, I don't think I've got a great deal of talent or ability. I started at the bottom and worked up.

> –Steve Jones, former marathon world record holder

405

There is something about the ritual of the race—putting on the number, lining up, being timed—that brings out the best in us.

> –Grete Waitz, the first woman in history to run the marathon in under 2.5 hours

406

Runner's don't die; they only smell like it.

> –Message printed on a runner's shirt

407

I believe in using races as motivators. It's hard to keep an exercise program if you don't have a significant goal in sight.

> –Bob Greene, American journalist and author

408

The man who has made the mile record is W.G. George.... His time is 4 minutes, 12.75 seconds, and the probability is that his record will never be beaten.

–Harry Andrews, in 1903

(*The current record for the mile, as of this writing, is 3 minutes, 43.13 seconds.*)

409

Running is a gift I give myself almost daily. Even on days when everything seems to go wrong, I treat myself to the satisfaction of a lap of 30 to 40 minutes.

–Arthur Blank, American businessman, co-founder of Home Depot

410

God grant me the courage not to give up even though I think it is hopeless.

–Chester W. Nimitz, Fleet Admiral of the U.S. Navy; assuming command at the most critical period of World War II in the Pacific, Admiral Nimitz organized his forces to halt the Japanese advance, despite the shortage of ships, planes, and supplies.

411

The Greeks saw man as a whole...mind/spirit/body. Developing each function made a person a harmonious whole. Running develops my body and creates that harmonious whole. Running is a place where my body is at home, a place where it does what it is meant to do and does it surprisingly well. Running is where I can become all I can be.

> –George Sheehan, physician, senior athlete, and author of many great books, in George Sheehan on Running to Win: How to Achieve the Physical, Mental & Spiritual Victories of Running

412

For me, as for so many runners, there really are no finish lines. Runs end; running doesn't.

> –Dean Karnazes, completed 50 marathons in 50 states on 50 consecutive days, author of *Ultramarathon Man: Confessions of an All-Night Runner*

413

My last race will finish at the casket. I'm going to jump in, close the lid and feel like I lived a full life.

> –Sid Howard, winner of 8 World Masters and 50 National Masters championships who is still running and coaching at age 80; as quoted in *Runspirations* by Amby Burfoot

414

I learned not to take the lead if I wasn't sure where the finish line was.

> –Pat Petersen, who got lost on his first cross country race

415

Hard work pays off. You have to be just as disciplined to run a business as you do to train for an athletic event.

–Wes Santee, an American middle-distance runner and athlete who competed mainly in the 1,500 meters and mile events.

416

I doubt if he'll ever be able to walk again.

–Doctor treating Glenn Cunningham when at age 7 he was badly burned in a fire; he later became the outstanding miler of his time

417

Don't let the fear of striking out hold you back.

–Babe Ruth, who once simultaneously held the records for striking out and for career home runs

418

There is nothing more certain than the defeat of the man who gives up.

–A cancer survivor turned runner

419

Life (and running) is not all about time but about our experiences along the way.

–Jen Rhines, American long-distance runner

420

When I am running, I feel everything is in sync. Even my mechanical leg becomes part of me.

–Sarah Reinertsen, American paratriathlete and former Paralympic track athlete

421

It's a beautiful day for it.

–Daily mantra of Wilbur Cross, Governor of Connecticut

(*He must have been talking about running, yes?*)

422

Everyone stumbles at one time or another. It's the human condition.

–Amby Burfoot, marathoner, author, and all-around good guy, in *The Runner's Guide to the Meaning of Life*

423

The highest reward for a person's toil is not what they get for it, but what they become of it.

 –John Ruskin, writer and philanthropist

424

But those who wait on the Lord shall renew their strength;
They shall mount up with wings like eagles;
They shall run and not be weary,
They shall walk and not faint.

 –Isaiah 40:31

425

The doctor said, "You're going to need stitches." She gave me a prescription to take three times a day for the pain. Then she asked if I had any questions. I replied, "So can I run tomorrow?"

 –Facebook meme

 (*But sounds like a runner!*)

426

Success is not to be pursued; it is to be attracted by the person you become.

> –Jim Rohn, entrepreneur, business philosopher, success coach, and author of more than thirty books, including *Leading an Inspired Life*

427

It's a treat being a runner, out in the world by yourself with not a soul to make you bad-tempered or tell you what to do.

> –Alan Sillitoe, British writer

428

There is no such thing as an average runner. If you are running, you're above average.

> –Overheard at a race

429

Running improves my relationships with my family, my friends, everyone around me. And while my running is personal, it's also something I give. Running can be given.

> –Tony Sandoval, M.D., winner of the 1980 U.S. Olympic Marathon Trials

430

If you believe in yourself and have the courage, the determination, the dedication, the competitive drive, and if you are willing to sacrifice the little things in life and pay the price for the things that are worthwhile, it can be done.

–Vince Lombardi, Superbowl-winning coach

431

I saw my times improving, and the more I did well, the more I wanted to see what was over the next ridge.

–Priscilla Welch, retired British marathon runner.

432

There are people who have no bodies, only heads. And many athletes have no heads, only bodies. A champion is a man who has trained his body and his mind, who has learned to conquer pain for his own purposes. A great athlete is at peace with himself and at peace with the world; he has fulfilled himself. He envies nobody.

–Coach Sam Dee

433

Long distance running is 90% mental and the other half is physical.

> –Rich Davis, men's cross-country coach at the University of Dayton for 18 seasons

434

My mascara runs faster than you do!

> –Message printed on the back of a runner's shirt

435

When I started running, I started dreaming. It couldn't be helped. The mind works as hard as the body does during exercise.

> –Bart Yasso, of the eponymous Yasso 800s workout, consisting of 10 x 800 meter runs; one of the few people to have completed races on all seven continents, including the Mount Kilimanjaro marathon, and who won the 1987 U.S. National Biathlon Long Course Championship

> (*Yasso 800s are considered a good predictor of your marathon time.*)

436

And while these pounds were being shed, while the physiological miracles were occurring with the heart and muscle and metabolism, psychological marvels were taking place as well. Just so, the world over, bodies, minds, and souls are constantly being born again, during miles on the road.

> –George Sheehan, physician, senior athlete, and author of many great books, in *Running to Win: How to Achieve the Physical, Mental, & Spiritual Victories of Running*

437

The hard part isn't getting your body in shape. The hard part is getting your mind in shape.

> –Amby Burfoot, marathoner, author, and all-around good guy

438

Part of a runner's training consists of pushing back the limits of his mind.

> –Kenny Moore, American journalist and athlete

439

I run because if I didn't, I'd be sluggish and glum and spend too much time on the couch. I run to breathe the fresh air. I run to explore. I run to escape the ordinary. I run...to savor the trip along the way. Life becomes a little more vibrant, a little more intense. I like that.

> –Dean Karnazes, completed 50 marathons in 50 states on 50 consecutive days, author of *Ultramarathon Man: Confessions of an All-Night Runner*

440

If it was easy, I would do it!

> –Message on a sign at a marathon

441

Running. the most expensive "free" sport out there!

> –Unknown

442

You gotta dig a little deeper. Find out who you are.

> –Unknown

443

I was determined to keep pace with a four-year old who was riding a Dora the Explorer bike with pink training wheels.

> –Diane Stark, on what helped motivate her to start running and finish the Not-So-Fun Run for charity with the second slowest time of all runners, in *Chicken Soup for the Soul: Running for Good: 101 Stories for Runners & Walkers to Get You Moving* by Amy Newmark and Dean Karnazes

444

Pressure is nothing more than the shadow of great opportunity.

-Michael Johnson, retired American sprinter

445

If you'd have kept that pace up, you'd have broken the national indoor record.

-Bill Meek, my high school track coach regarding my first quarter in my first high-school race, an indoor mile

(After that first quarter I was leading the pack at 59 seconds. I finished dead last by 100 yards. Translation: "You went out too fast"—without the sympathy.)

446

I was never any good at running. Glancing around...I realized that I actually fit in. There was no minimum speed or mileage requirement, no uniform body type.

-Karyn Curtis, after she started running with a group and later ran a number of marathons and ultramarathons, in *Chicken Soup for the Soul: Running for Good: 101 Stories for Runners & Walkers to Get You Moving* by Amy Newmark and Dean Karnazes

447

I developed a life motto. "Keep on moving on." We're all here to discover our life's purpose. Once we do, for Heaven's sake, get on with it.

> –Grace Butcher, national champion runner, as quoted in *Runspirations* by Amby Burfoot

448

"Why aren't you signed up for the 401(k)?"

"I'd never be able to run that far."

> –Scott Adams, in *Dilbert* (4/2/2001)

449

Every achiever I have ever met says, "My life turned around when I began to believe in me."

> –Robert Schuller, American Christian televangelist, pastor, motivational speaker, and author

450

Never stop hoping for more, expecting the best, pushing harder and celebrating early and often.

> –Marc Parent, author of *The Newbie Chronicles* in *Runner's World* magazine

451

I think about the simplistic idea of powering one's body with nothing more than willpower. No gears, no chains, no wheels, no paddles—just 100% dedication to the concept of forward motion. In my opinion there is no movement more pure.

> –Jon Penfold, runner, in *Chicken Soup for the Soul: Running for Good: 101 Stories for Runners & Walkers to Get You Moving* by Amy Newmark and Dean Karnazes

452

Success means having the courage, the determination and the will to become the person you were meant to be.

> –George Sheehan, physician, senior athlete, and author of many great books, including *Running & Being: The Total Experience*

453

When a person really desires something, all the universe conspires to help that person to realize his dream.

> –Paul Coelho, author of *The Alchemist: A Fable About Following Your Dream*

454

There is something magical about running; after a certain distance it transcends the body. Then a bit further, it transcends the mind.

> –Kristen Armstrong, former professional road bicycle racer and three-time Olympic gold medalist

455

Nobody running at full speed has either a head or a body.

> –William Butler Yeats, Irish poet and playwright

456

Those who try to do something and fail...are infinitely better than those who try to do nothing and succeed.

> –Lloyd Jones, Welsh Protestant theologian and doctor

457

March on. Do not tarry. To go forward is to move toward perfection. March on, and fear not the thorns, or the sharp stones on life's path.

> –Khalil Gibran, writer, poet, and artist

458

There's a moment in every race. A moment where you can either quit, fold, or say to yourself, "I can do it!"

> –Jerry Lynch, who played baseball from 1954 to 1966 for the Pittsburgh Pirates and Cincinnati Reds

459

Yet that man is happy and poets sing of him who conquers with hand and swift foot and strength.

> –Pindar, Greek poet around 500 B.C.

460

When you have the enthusiasm and the passion, you end up figuring how to excel.

–Deena Kastor, U.S. Olympic marathoner

461

Our running shoes have magic in them. The power to transform a bad day into a good day; frustration into speed; self-doubt into confidence; chocolate cake into muscle.

–Mina Samuels, in *Run Like a Girl: How Strong Women Make Happy Lives*

462

I was looking for God during that last mile, but I didn't see him. I guess He finished ahead of me too.

–Albert Mabus, after finishing last at the 2001 Nittany Valley Half-Marathon

463

Hard days and slow miles come to all of us, but we keep running. If we draw on the people around us, we can all finish strong.

> -Kate E. Anderson, in *Chicken Soup for the Soul: Running for Good: 101 Stories for Runners & Walkers to Get You Moving* by Amy Newmark and Dean Karnazes

464

Motivation remains the key to the marathon: the motivation to begin, the motivation to continue, the motivation never to quit.

> -Hal Higdon, American distance runner and author of more than 36 books, including *Marathon: The Ultimate Training Guide*

465

Running together makes friendships stronger and stronger.

> -Chrisje Taesendonck
>
> (*Running friends are loyal, real, and there for you.*)

466

Don't give up.

> –Brian Fleming, a former alcoholic and video game addict who has dropped 390 pounds—so far—and who inspires others to turn their lives around through running

467

Running will welcome you, no matter how highly incapable you've been at sports. Give it a chance to do that.

> –Dana L. Ayers, in *Confessions of an Unlikely Runner: A Guide to Racing and Obstacle Courses for the Averagely Fit and Halfway Dedicated*

468

You've never met Dan Berlin.

> –Charles Scott, a blind running guide, to local authorities when they said a blind person couldn't track up the Inca Trail, one of the toughest treks in the world.
>
> (*Dan did it in 13 hours, the first blind athlete to do so.*)

469

If you run every day until you're 90 years old, I guarantee that you'll live a long life.

 –Bill Rogers, in *Lifetime Running Plan*

470

Never limit where running can take you. I mean that geographically, spiritually, and, of course, physically.

–Bart Yasso, of the eponymous Yasso 800s workout, consisting of 10 x 800 meter runs; one of the few people to have completed races on all seven continents, including the Mount Kilimanjaro marathon, and who won the 1987 U.S. National Biathlon Long Course Championship.

> (*Yasso 800s are considered a good predictor of your marathon time.*)

471

Are my kids still chasing me?

 –Message printed on the back of a runner's shirt

472

Labor and delivery was easier than this.

 –Message printed on a male runner's shirt.

> (*The man had more conversations with women at a race than I have ever seen. Not all were upbeat and positive, by the way.*)

473

You have no idea how strong you are, you think you can't do it, you think you're going to die, but I promise you, if you just stick with it, you realize that you had it in you the entire time.

-Jillian Michaels, American author.

474

A good run is good for your perspective, getting you beyond the bad, the worse, or even the downright apocalyptic. Live the way you run. Run happy.

-Advertisement for Brooks athletic wear

475

Yabba Dabba Doo!

-Fred Flintstone, of *The Flintstones, Town of Bedrock*, running and happy

476

I am not judged by the number of times I fail, but by the number of times I succeed. And the number of times I succeed is in direct proportion to the number of times I fail and keep trying.

-Tom Hopkins, professional sales trainer

477

5:37:43

- Fastest marathon on crutches on one leg

(*Recorded by Larry Chloupek II.*)

478

On longer runs in the countryside, carry some TP.

- Steve Williams, runner, on the toughest lesson he's learned as a runner

479

If it can't be today, maybe tomorrow. If it can't be tomorrow, maybe next week. If not next week, then maybe next month. With relentless focus and hard work, it will come.

- Meb Keflezighi, retired Eritrean-born American long-distance runner

480

I figured that if I was going to be telling people to get healthy, I should get healthy.

-Adam Kobialka, a medical resident who started running, dropped 50 pounds, and ran a marathon in 3:01

481

We must all wage an intense, lifelong battle against the constant downward pull. If we relax, the bugs and weeds of negativity will move into the garden and take everything we value.

-Jim Rohn, entrepreneur, business philosopher, success coach, and author of more than thirty books, including *Leading an Inspired Life*

482

Running allows you to set your mind free. Nothing seems impossible. Nothing unattainable.

-Kara Goucher, who made her marathon debut in 2008 and finished third the following year at the Boston Marathon.

483

It could all end tomorrow, so enjoy what you have and never take it for granted. And never forget to take an easy run for yourself once in a while and just remember why you love to run.

–Dathan Ritzenhein, Athletics competitor

484

Most of us have enough areas in our lives where we have to meet others' expectations. Let your running be about your own hopes and dreams.

–Meb Keflezighi, who won the silver medal in the 2004 Olympics marathon and finished fourth in 2012

485

I can make a comeback if George Foreman can.

–Said Aouita, Moroccan runner who won the 5,000 meter at the Olympics and at the Athletics World Championships

486

A runner must run with dreams in his heart, not money in his pocket.

–Emil Zatopek, Olympic long-distance runner

487

I don't know how the creative process works, but it always seems, when I'm running...that thoughts start coming in.

-Robert Caro, biographer

488

It's your run. It's all up to you.

-Kevin Nelson in *The Runner's Book of Daily Inspiration: A Year of Motivation, Revelation, and Instruction*

489

Every calling is great, when greatly pursued.

-Oliver Wendell Holmes, United States Supreme Court Justice

490

I'm afraid that if I give up running, I'll have to replace it with murder.

-Unknown

491

Joanie, if marathons make you look like this, please don't run anymore.

  -Olympic marathoner Joan Benoit's mom, after seeing a newspaper photo of her at the finish line

  (*Note to self: Look good at the finish line no matter how you feel.*)

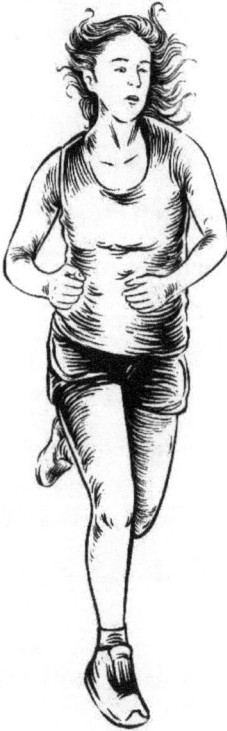

492

All runners are tough. Everyone has to have a little fire in them, that even in tough times can't be turned off."

–Shalane Flanagan, Olympic long-distance runner

493

If you can fill the unforgiving minute

With sixty seconds' worth of distance run,

Yours is the Earth and everything that's in it,

And—which is more—you'll be a Man, my son!

–Rudyard Kipling, in his poem "If—"

494

Every time I fail, I assume I will be a stronger person for it. I keep on running figuratively and literally, despite a limp that gets more noticeable with each passing season, because for me there has always been a place to go and a terrible urgency to get there.

–Joan Benoit Samuelson, first Olympic women's marathon winner, who also held the fastest time for an American woman at the Chicago Marathon for 32 years after winning the race in 1985

495

If it is 45 degrees outside and you think that is optimal—
you might be a runner.

-Unknown

496

Happiness is a brand new pair of running shoes.

-Unknown

497

My fastest times may be behind me, but my best self is yet
to come.

-Deena Kastor, Olympic long-distance runner

498

Go ahead, every once in a while and jump into that puddle
with both feet. It takes conscious thought to keep play in
our running.

-John Jerome author of
The Elements of Effort:
Reflections on the Art
and Science of Running

499

I think the idea of a two-hour marathon is thoroughly ridiculous. Absolutely ridiculous.

> –Derek Clayton, Australian long-distance runner, who on December 3, 1967, was the first to break 2 hours and 10 minutes in the marathon

I don't believe in limits.

> –Marathoner Eliud Kipchoge, marathon runner, on breaking the 2-hour barrier on October 12, 2019

500

Wake up, say thanks, and go run.

> –Michael D'Aulerio, author of *A Runner's Secret: One Run Will Get It Done*

501

Running changed everything. It got me out of my rut, helped me lose 55 pounds, and taught me in life you should give more than you take. I never had a bad run.

> –Mike Monestime, father of two, training for a marathon while in grad school and working a full-time job

502

It is better to look ahead and prepare than to look back and regret.

> –Jackie Joyner-Kersee, retired Olympic track and field athlete

503

If you have ever said, "I only ran 5 miles today"—you might be a runner.

> –Adapted from a Facebook meme

504

I'll be happy if running and I can grow old together.

> –Haruki Marakami, a writer with bestsellers in Japan as well as internationally, author of *What I Talk About When I Talk About Running*

505

Dad, when we were running, I felt like I wasn't disabled anymore.

> –Rick Hoyt, severely disabled since birth, to his dad, Dick Hoyt, who swam (with Rick in a raft), biked (with Rick in a side car), and ran (with Rick in a pushcart) an Ironman Triathlon
>
> (*An amazing story. For more, visit the website TeamHoyt.com.*)

506

Running along the beach at sunrise with no other footprints in the sand, you realize the vastness of creation, your own insignificant space in the plan...your own creatureliness and how much you owe to the supreme body, the God that brought all this beauty and harmony into being.

-Sister Marion Irvine, nun and marathon runner

507

They can conquer who believe they can.

-Virgil, around 20 BC

508

There are those of us who are always about to live. We are waiting until things change, until there is more time, until we are less tired, until we get a promotion, until we settle down ... until, until, until. It always seems as if there is some major event that must occur in our lives before we begin living.

> -George Sheehan, physician, senior athlete, and author of many great books, including *Running & Being: The Total Experience*

509

If you have more patience running for an hour than waiting 5 minutes in Walmart—you might be a runner.

> -Adapted from a Facebook meme

510

If you need help getting motivated, turn to fellow runners. Often, they have been there, done that, and can help move you along.

> -Hal Higdon, American distance runner, author of more than 36 books, including *Marathon: The Ultimate Training Guide*

511

The average American takes twenty years to get out of condition and he wants to get back in condition in twenty days—and you just can't do it.

—Kenneth Cooper, physician and founder of the Cooper Institute, who logged more than 38,000 miles of running at age 88, and became known as the "father of aerobics"

512

You can't talk yourself into shape. Either you can do it or you can't.

—Frank Shorter, American long-distance runner, Olympic gold medalist

513

If you have a conflict or problem in your life and you think, "I need to go for a run"—you might be a runner.

—Adapted from a Facebook meme

514

Make the expectation lively enough, and action will follow.

—Mason Cooley, American academic

515

Running was supposed to collapse my uterus.

> –Katherine Switzer, the first woman to officially finish the Boston Marathon, on a common belief, at the time, on why women shouldn't run long distances

516

My lover has the most beautiful body in the world. Because she runs. I fell in love with her because she had the most beautiful body I had ever seen.

> –Sara Maitland in *The Loveliness of the Long-Distance Runner*

517

Knowing is not enough; we must apply.

Willing is not enough; we must do.
> –Johann Wolfgang von Goethe, German prolific writer and statesman, around 1830

518

I'm overwhelmed by the strength of my body and the power of my mind. For one moment, just one second, I feel immortal.

> –Diana Nyad, an American author, journalist, motivational speaker, and long-distance swimmer

519

Whenever I go running, I meet new people. Like paramedics.

–Facebook meme

520

Action is character.

–F. Scott Fitzgerald, American novelist and screenwriter

521

Is there anything worse than pressing pause on your running watch and forgetting to press resume during your run?

–Unknown

522

If you are losing faith in human nature, go out and watch a marathon.

>   -Katherine Switzer, the first woman Boston Marathoner, before women were allowed to enter

>   *(She put "K. Switzer" on her entry form.)*

523

First you feel like dying. Then you feel reborn.

>   -Advertisement for Asics athletic wear

524

Change your life today. Don't gamble on the future, act now without delay!

>   -Simone de Beauvoir, French writer

525

There's not one body type that equates to success. Access the body you have and be the best you can be with it.

>   -Mary Sullen

526

The world is your treadmill. Run all over it.

>   -Pinterest meme

527

Dear God: If you have a plan for my life, please show up sooner than later because things aren't going so well.

> –Jim Ryun, after being cut from his junior high school baseball team, as quoted in *Runspirations: Amazing Stories, Timeless Wisdom, and Motivational Quotes to Help You Run Stronger Every Day* by Amby Burfoot and Gail Kislevitz
>
> *(Ryun later started to run track, and was the first high-school miler to break the four-minute-mile barrier.)*

528

As long as my body can stay upright I'll compete. I run for the sheer enjoyment of being able to run. And I thank God every day for my health and that I can still run.

> –Chuck Milliman, who at age 85 ran an 85-mile run

529

It's good therapy. Running has always been a good way to get out ahead of everything.

> –Ernest Andrus, age 91, who ran his first 200-mile relay at the age of 88
>
> *(He liked it so much he ran three more.)*

530

Don't do anything new on race day.

-A runner's commandment, original author unknown

531

You've got to have faith.... Faith is believing.... After a certain point you've made your decision and prepared as much as you can. All that's left is to take a deep breath and step into the unknown.

-Mark Remy, in his article "Twenty Years, Twenty Lessons" in *Runner's World* magazine

532

My running style has been described as startled gazelle.

-Overheard on race day

533

Running has made me respect the human body and know what it's capable of achieving. I want to help others discover that and reach their goals.

-Zach Moran, who as a defensive lineman in football had never run more than 10 yards, then started running, lost 90 pounds, and ran a half marathon in 1 hour and 37 minutes

534

Because she's seen you do this today, she's going to grow up thinking she can run a marathon.

> –A mom who has a daughter with Down's syndrome, to Megan Thomas, a marathon runner who has a learning disability, and to her guide runner, Sarah Jones, at the London Marathon

(Who are you motivating? Who will you be?)

535

I have Crohn's disease, a chronic illness. The flares are unpredictable, so it's hard to plan a running goal. So the way I measure success is simple: Did I run today? Running gives me such an emotional release, so if I'm healthy enough to run, that, to me, is the greatest success. It's the ultimate privilege.

> –Allison Feller, runner

536

When I look at a pair of my massive old trousers that I still keep in my wardrobe, I can hardly believe I was once that big before I began running.... I've lost more than half my weight because of running and eating right.

> –Ed Horton, runner

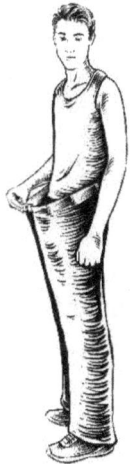

537

Some people might say going for a run is running away from your problems, but I feel it's very positive. It's going towards them to address them head on. Running has made me who I am today.... Running saved my life.

> –Jessica Morgan, who was sexually assaulted at 19, and while fighting through depression started running and counseling. She went on to say, "Running saved my life."

538

Everyone runs for a reason. Some of us run towards goals; others run to overcome obstacles. We run to prove others wrong or prove ourselves right. At times, I run to clear my mind and forget; other times, I run to remember.... My husband runs when the Air Force tells him he has to.

> –Tammi Keen, in *Chicken Soup for the Soul: Running for Good: 101 Stories for Runners & Walkers to Get You Moving* by Amy Newmark and Dean Karnazes

539

The runner who finishes last gets the most value out of their entry fee.

> –Facebook meme

540

It's time.

-Advertisement from the Montana Office of Tourism

(I take it as a reminder that now is the time to do what I need to do.)

541

Don't forget to cheer for yourself when you reach the finish line.

-Charmaine J. Forde, author of *Over in Away: A Collection of Stories and Poems*

542

My wife tells me, "That's not good for you!" and I ask her, "Can you run a half-marathon?"

-Ernest Andrus, 91, half marathoner who still runs 18 miles in a week, on his enjoyment of his usual breakfast of biscuits and gravy with vanilla milk

543

Believe that you can run farther and faster. Believe that you're young enough, old enough, strong enough, and so on, to accomplish everything you want to do. Don't let worn-out beliefs stop you from moving beyond yourself.

> -John Bingham, one of the most widely quoted runners and a great writer himself, author of *The Courage to Start: A Guide to Running for Your Life*

544

What seems hard today will one day be your warmup.

> -Unknown

545

Let him that would move the world, first move himself.

> -Socrates, ancient Greek philosopher

546

If your running shoes are the most expensive shoes you own-you might be a runner.

> -Adapted from a Facebook meme

547

I say I'm going to finish last. That takes the pressure off.

-Dan Middleman, American long-distance runner

548

I don't drive a car. I drive a portable locker room.

-One runner to another as he opened his trunk, which was filled with running gear and sporting equipment

549

Some might say it's easier to be a runner than the runner's family.

-Robert de Castella, Australian long-distance runner

550

If you want to be happy, set a goal that commands your thoughts, liberates your energy, and inspires your hopes.

-Andrew Carnegie, the richest American in the 19th century

551

It's not so much that I began to run, but that I continued.

> -Hal Higdon, American distance runner, author of more than 36 books, including *Marathon: The Ultimate Training Guide*

552

Who will you be?

> -Advertisement for Dick's Sporting Goods

553

Sometimes people will say to me, "Oprah's got it easy because she's got a personal trainer and a personal chef." But that's baloney. No one can run for you. She was on the track every morning.

> -Bob Greene, Oprah Winfrey's personal trainer

> *(Oprah kept training and eventually ran a marathon—and actually ran the whole distance, never walked a step.)*

554

Running has brought balance into my life, it's brought me back to the things I almost lost. Now I can be that father, that person I've always wanted to be.

> –David Clark, who had been a drug addict weighing 320 pounds, then one day said, "I quit" and started running, lost 160 pounds, and got his life back

555

Two bombers tried to destroy me and instead they made me stronger.

> –Rebekah Gregory, who lost her leg in the Boston Marathon bombing, and went on to become a runner with the help of a prosthetic leg

556

You're going to hit times when you really feel that you're crazy. You have to push through that.

> –Gregory Castle, who at 72 became the oldest person to ever complete the 170 mile Grand to Grand Ultra

557

In the school's races, I always ran my legs off. There were girls watching and I wanted to impress them.

> –Juha Vaatainen, two-time European Championship gold medal winner, on why he ran in school

558

I started running to get a letter jacket, a girlfriend.

> –Jim Ryun, Olympian and first American high schooler to break the 4-minute-mile barrier

> *(Know your "why"!)*

559

The man who is in the state of running, of continuous running into peace, is a heavenly man. He continually runs and moves and seeks peace in running.

> –Meister Eckhart, German theologian

560

That's what I want to convey. You can do this, but you're going to have to work for it.

> –Marla Runyam, who in 2000 was the first legally blind person to compete in the Olympic games, and finished 8th in the 1500-meter event

561

There are many reasons for running as there are days in the year. But mostly I run because I am an animal and a child, an artist and a saint. So, too, are you.

> –George Sheehan, physician, senior athlete, and author of many great books, including *Running & Being: The Total Experience*

562

The reason I exercise is for the quality of life I enjoy.

> –Kenneth Cooper, physician and founder of the Cooper Institute, who logged more than 38,000 miles of running at age 88, and became known as the "father of aerobics"

563

After all, if you run far enough, no one can catch you.

> –V.E. Schwab, an American fantasy author best known for her 2013 novel *Vicious*, the Shades of Magic series, and for her children's and young adult fiction published under the name Victoria Schwab

564

Continuous effort—not strength or intelligence—is the key to unlocking our potential.

-Winston Churchill, former British Prime Minister

565

I've caught a few breaks, but God likes me and I like Him, too. My philosophy is: I just put one foot in front of the other and keep going.

-John A. "Old John" Kelley, 1957 Boston Marathon winner

566

Not only in running but in much of life is a sense of balance and proportion necessary.

-Clarence DeMar, 7-time Boston Marathon winner

567

You can't find your strong if you're not looking for it.

-Advertisement for Saucony athletic gear

568

It eluded us, but that's no matter. Tomorrow we will run faster.

-F. Scott Fitzgerald, American author

569

You can get through this. If I can, anyone can. Actually, did I ever tell you about the time I ran a marathon?

...When race day arrived, I realized my task had become something greater. I was running for that young, frail, bald man in a chemo chair next to mine and his twenty-something wife sitting quietly next to him and hiding her tears...I was running for everyone who has heard the words, "you have cancer."

> –Joan Donnelly-Emery, on her thoughts during a marathon she completed in 5½ hours after being told, "You have cancer," in *Chicken Soup for the Soul: Running for Good: 101 Stories for Runners & Walkers to Get You Moving* by Amy Newmark and Dean Karnazes

570

You are truly your own hero in running. It is up to you to have the responsibility and self-discipline to get the job done.

> –Adam Goucher, who ran the 5,000-meter event for the United States at the 2000 Olympics

571

Your personal philosophy is the greatest determining factor in how your life works out.

> –Jim Rohn, Success Coach, author of the book, *7 Strategies of Wealth and Happiness*

572

The best motivation is self-motivation. The guy says, "I wish someone would come by and turn me on." What if they don't show up? You've got to have a better plan for your life.

> -Jim Rohn, entrepreneur, business philosopher, success coach, and author of more than thirty books, including *Leading an Inspired Life*

573

I once ran thirty-one miles, and after that there was nothing in the world I couldn't do.

> -Katherine Switzer, the first woman to officially finish the Boston Marathon

574

You can't wait for inspiration. You have to go after it with a club.

> -Jack London, American author, journalist, and social activist

575

Run like there's a hot guy in front of you and a creepy dude behind you.

–Message printed on a runner's shirt

576

If one has determination, then things will get done.

–Chinese Proverb

577

Even when you've gone as far as you can, and you're staring at the specter of self-doubt, you can find a bit more strength deep inside you.

–Hal Higdon, American distance runner, author of more than 36 books, including *Marathon: The Ultimate Training Guide*

578

They say you can't run away from your troubles. I say that you can.

–John Bingham, one of the most widely quoted runners and a great writer himself, author of *The Courage to Start: A Guide to Running for Your Life*

579

Success or failure depends more upon attitude than upon capacity. Act, look, feel successful, conduct yourself accordingly, and you will be amazed at the results.

-William James, Harvard physician and psychologist

(Turn back to quote #111 to see one of my all-time favorite quotes, also from William James.)

580

Looking forward to something is much more fun than looking back at something—and much more constructive.

-Hortense Odlum, American businesswoman

581

If you're in a bad mood, go for a walk. If you're still in a bad mood, go for a run.

-Hippocrates, paraphrased

582

God grant me the strength to travel this distance, the courage to push through the pain and the wisdom to know when to pick up the pace. Without your guidance and understanding, I could not be the runner I am. Amen.

-Runner's prayer, original author unknown

583

In the 30 years I've been a runner. I've run more than 150,000 miles. Still, some of the hardest steps I take are those first few getting out the door for the daily runs.

> –Bill Rodgers, in *Bill Rodgers' Lifetime Running Plan: Definitive Programs for Runners of All Ages and Levels*

584

Those who turned back never reached the summit.

> –H. Jackson Brown, in Life's Instructions for Wisdom, Success and Happiness

585

Remember the feeling you get from a good run is far better than the feeling you get sitting around wishing you were running.

> –Sarah Condor, New York City Marathoner runner

586

Live your life each day as you would climb a mountain. An occasional glance towards the summit keeps the goal in mind, but many beautiful scenes are observed from each new vantage point. Climb slowly, steadily, enjoying each passing moment; The view from the summit will serve as a fitting climax for the journey.

-Harold V. Melchert

587

The discipline it took to train has entered all facets of my life. I am more focused, get more done during the day.

-Matthew Shafner

588

If you see me collapse, please pause my watch.

-Message printed on a runner's shirt

589

Run the mile you're in.

-Ryan Hall, World Athletics competitor

(This reminds me of the maxim, "Wherever you go, be there.")

590

It's not about speed and gold medals. It's about refusing to be stopped.

> –Amby Burfoot, marathoner, author, and all-around good guy, author of *The Runner's Guide to the Meaning of Life*

591

My grandmother started walking five miles a day when she was 60. She's 97 now, and we don't know where the heck she is.

> –Ellen DeGeneres, American comedian, television host, actress, writer, and producer

592

It's highly unlikely. There are walkers.

> –Overheard at a 5k race when a new runner said, "I'm afraid I'll finish last."

593

In truth, after having friends die too young, I'm thankful to be here, enjoy life, and see my kids grow up.

> –Blake Russell, Olympic marathoner, on learning that her husband expected a meltdown on her 40th birthday

594

I plan to be running as long as I can, and have no plans to stop.

> –Frank Shorter, 1972 Olympic marathon gold medalist, now age 75 and still running

595

If you want to go running with me, you'd better be prepared to walk a lot.

> –Message printed on a runner's shirt

596

Work harder on yourself than you do on your job.

> –Jim Rohn, entrepreneur, business philosopher, success coach, and author of more than thirty books, including Leading an Inspired Life

597

Your problems will seem more manageable. Your work will be more productive. Your thinking will be clearer. You will be more tuned in to your relationships. Your emotional state of being will be richer and fuller.

> –Kevin Nelson, on the benefits of running, in *The Runner's Book of Daily Inspirations: A Year of Motivation, Revelation, and Instruction*

598

Good Luck. I love you. Don't die.

> –Madilynn Winters, 13-year-old daughter of Amy Palmiero-Winters, offering words of encouragement right before her mom's 140-mile race in the Sahara Desert, in *Runspirations: Amazing Stories, Timeless Wisdom, and Motivational Quotes to Help You Run Stronger Every Day* by Amby Burfoot and Gail Kislevitz

599

Run when I can, walk when I cannot run, and creep when I cannot walk.

> –John Bunyan in The Pilgrim's Progress

600

Good physical training is important. But what goes on in your head will determine whether you'll win or lose, whether you'll be able to break through a psychological barrier or not—and whether you'll hold a medal in your hands and smile with satisfaction at the end.

> –Tim Noakes, sports researcher

601

Find a group of people who challenge and inspire you; spend a lot of time with them and it will change your life.

-Amy Poehler, American actress

602

Don't be a jogger. They're the ones who find the bodies.

-Message printed on a runner's shirt

603

Tough runs don't last. Tough runners do.

-Advertisement for Saucony athletic gear

604

I live for those last moments in a race. It's why I run. It's ecstasy and insanity. It's freedom. For a few moments, I can fly.

-Olivia O'Toole, Irish footballer

605

Don't waste life in doubts and fears; spend yourself on the work before you, well assured that the right performance of this hour's duties will be the best preparation for the hours and ages that will follow it.

> –Ralph Waldo Emerson, American essayist, lecturer, and philosopher

606

Never let the odds keep you from pursuing what you know in your heart you were meant to do.

> –H. Jackson Brown, in *Life's Instructions for Wisdom, Success and Happiness*

607

Nothing can stop the man with the right mental attitude from achieving his goal, nothing on earth can help the man with the wrong mental attitude.

> –Thomas Jefferson, third President of the United States

608

Like the marathon, life can sometimes be difficult, challenging, and present obstacles, however if you believe in your dreams and never ever give up, things will turn out for the best.

> –Meb Keflezighi, U.S. Olympic silver medalist in the marathon, who also won both the New York City Marathon and the Boston Marathon

609

Running helps extend my "never killed anyone" streak.

> –Message printed on a runner's shirt

610

Believe you can do it. Think no other way but "Yes you can." The human body is capable of considerably more physical endurance than most of us realize.

> –Paul Reese, a United States Marine Corps colonel during World War II

611

Most people never run far enough on their first wind to find out they've got a second.

> –William James, American philosopher, psychologist, and pragmatist

612

One of the best places to start to turn your life around is doing what appears on your mental, "I should" list.

–Jim Rohn, entrepreneur, business philosopher, success coach, and author of more than thirty books, including *Leading an Inspired Life*

613

First with the head and then with the heart, that's how a man stays ahead from the start.

–Bryce Courtenay, in *The Power of One*

614

Runners are a different breed. We take pride in blistered feet, bruised toenails, and chafed skin. We become experts in energy gels and hydration strategies. For many of us, running is a refuge from day-to-day stress. It's our passion. Our meditation and reflection. We run to live and live to run.

–Nancy Girard, runner, *iRun* magazine contributor

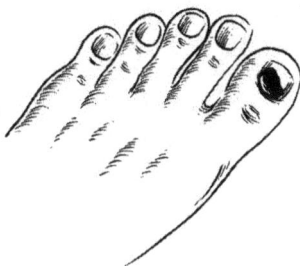

615

The old man asked me what I was running from. I was in full stride, so I couldn't slow down to answer him. I could only hope that the wind carried my correction of "running toward" to his ears.

> –Nancy LaMar Rodgers, therapist and wellness coach

> *(Be a "run toward" person!)*

616

A good laugh and a long run are life's best medicines.

> –Unknown

617

I run because I don't have enough control to stop emotional eating.

> –Unknown

618

It's not what you are that holds you back, it's what you think you are not.

> –Denis Waitley, author of the classic book *The Psychology of Winning: Ten Qualities of a Total Winner*

619

I may look awkward running. You look awkward sitting on the couch. Do you want to bet who fits in smaller pants first?

-Unknown

620

When we can no longer change a situation, we are challenged to change ourselves.

-Victor Frankl, author of one of the best life-changing books ever, *Man's Search for Meaning*

621

For someone who runs all the time, I still have the ability to make it look like it's the first time I've ever tried.

-Overheard from a seasoned runner before a long run

622

Sometimes you will never know the value of a moment until it becomes a memory.

-Theodor Seuss Geigel, a.k.a. "Dr. Seuss," American children's writer and illustrator

623

Daddy, why did Mommy run by our house?

Because she misjudged the distance of her long run, so she can't come home until her GPS watch tells her it's OK.

-Facebook meme

624

There are times when you run a marathon and you wonder, "Why am I doing this?" But you take a drink of water, and around the next bend you get your wind back, remember the finish line, and keep going.

-Steve Jobs, the late CEO of Apple

625

Wisely and slowly. They stumble that run fast.

-William Shakespeare, in *Romeo and Juliet*

626

The first person you have to inspire every day is yourself. Running will do that.

-Marc Parent, *Runner's World* columnist

627

It's the road signs, "Beware of lions."

> –Kip Lagat, Kenyan distance runner, on why his country produces so many great runners

628

A 12-minute mile is just as far as a 6-minute mile.

> –Message printed on a poster

629

Your work is to discover your world and then with all your heart give yourself to it.

> –The Buddha

630

Running won't kill you. You'll pass out first.

> –Message printed on a runner's shirt

631

Simply believing you can do something has pretty powerful perks. For one, you're more likely to stick with a commitment when things get tough.

> -Cindra Kamphoff, professor of sports psychology, trainer, high performance coach, and author of *Beyond Grit: Ten Powerful Practices to Gain the High-Performance Edge*
>
> *(Do you believe?)*

632

There are few greater feelings in this world than when you have only one mile to go and your favorite running song comes on.

> -Overheard at the finish line of a half marathon from a runner who finished well, smiling

633

Make no little plans, they have no magic to stir men's blood.... Make big plans, aim high in hope and work.

> -Daniel H. Burnham, American architect and urban designer

634

Take action. All your planning and dreaming is useless unless you do.

-H. Jackson Brown, in *Life's Instructions for Wisdom, Success and Happiness*

635

In the end, the real difference between the people who get what they truly want and the people that don't is commitment—the determination to move relentlessly toward a desire.... Commitment isn't one action, it's many. So, commit early, commit often.

-Dan Clements and Tara Gignac in *Escape 101: The Four Secrets to Taking a Sabbatical or Career Break Without Losing Your Money or Your Mind*

636

Unless commitment is made, there are only promises and hopes...but no plans.

-Peter Drucker, business consulting guru and author of *The Effective Executive: The Definitive Guide to Getting the Right Things Done*

637

It's never too late in life to have a genuine adventure.

–Robert Kurson, American writer

(Ready to start your new adventure?)

638

"What Is Success?"

To laugh often and much;
To win the respect of intelligent people
and the affection of children;
To earn the approbation of honest critics
and endure the betrayal of false friends;
To appreciate beauty;
To find the best in others;
To leave the world a bit better, whether by a healthy child,
a garden patch, or a redeemed social condition;
To know even one life has breathed easier
because you have lived–
This is to have succeeded.

> –Bessie Stanley (often incorrectly attributed to Ralph Waldo Emerson)

Randy L. Thurman, CPA, CFP®, and a runner

Randy Thurman is a runner, but it didn't start out that way. Turning fifty, and starting to look like a pear, motivated him to do something, so he started running and hasn't stopped since. It's been twelve years now and he is healthier, has more energy, and his overall attitude has improved (see quotes #25 and #46), all because of running.

In his professional life, Randy is a CPA and a CERTIFIED FINANCIAL PLANNER™. He runs a fee-only investment advisory practice in Oklahoma City, Oklahoma, with 20 employees. Randy finds many parallels between running a marathon, long-term investment success, and life in general, but he tells us he'll wait to share that wisdom on another day.

Pati, his wife, is a triathlete. Randy has considered doing a tri, but for some reason the officials won't allow him to swim with floaties on. His son, Levi, hasn't fallen in love with running as his mom and dad have, but he is into Jiu-Jitsu. He's currently a purple belt and competes at the expert level. Randy and Pati hope he will continue with Jiu-Jitsu as a lifelong sport.